THE SOUP HAS MANY EYES

From Shtetl to Chicago

A Memoir

of One

Family's Journey

Through History

BANTAM BOOKS
New York   Toronto
London   Sydney   Auckland

THE

SOUP

HAS

MANY

EYES

Joann Rose Leonard

THE SOUP HAS MANY EYES

A Bantam Book / March 2000

All rights reserved.
Copyright © 2000 by Joann Rose Leonard.

BOOK DESIGN BY GLEN M. EDELSTEIN.

Library of Congress Cataloging-in-Publication Data
Leonard, Joann Rose.
The soup has many eyes : from shtetl to Chicago : a memoir of one family's journey through history / Joann Rose Leonard.
p.   cm.
ISBN 0-553-80159-7
1. Leonard, Joann Rose—Family.   2. Jews—Illinois—Chicago Biography.
3. Leonard family.   4. Chicago (Ill.) Biography.   5. Leonard, Joann Rose Anecdotes.
6. Jews—Illinois—Chicago Anecdotes.   7. Chicago (Ill.) Anecdotes.   I. Title.
F548.9.J5L46   2000
977.3'1104'0922—dc21
[B]   99-39229
                                                              CIP

Published simultaneously in the United States and Canada

Bantam Books are published by Bantam Books, a division of Random House, Inc. Its trademark, consisting of the words "Bantam Books" and the portrayal of a rooster, is Registered in U.S. Patent and Trademark Office and in other countries. Marca Registrada. Bantam Books, 1540 Broadway, New York, New York 10036.

PRINTED IN THE UNITED STATES OF AMERICA

RRH   10   9   8   7   6   5   4   3   2   1

THE SOUP HAS MANY EYES

Dearest Joshua and Jonathan,

*W*hen you were babies, my hand could cover your back, the whole of it, from the nape of your neck to the dimples just above your rump cheeks. You were warm loaves of new-made bread radiating potential. And I, the most satisfied of all possible cooks, fed you from my own body, flesh to flesh.

Through the old wavy glass of the nursery window, the seasons blurred into Monet landscapes. But inside, we held time at bay, rocking away from the moment over and over. I burped you and tucked you into your crib. Yet when I peeked in a short while later, I was stunned with what I found. You had slipped away—skeined out like kite string, farther and farther, the unseen weight of time and distance bowing your long, tenuous tether as you soared and dove in the blue.

Josh, you left behind a pair of tie-dyed jeans, a hand-painted winged creature on the thigh—apt emblem for your explorer's spirit that chafed at confines even before birth. Acrobatic and restless, you trampolined against the walls of my womb, and once born, from the very first hour you scooched on your belly to the top of your hospital bassinet. There you wailed, fierce, red-faced, head butted against the hard plastic, until the nurse came and pulled you back down. Over and over, you repeated this skirmish to the edge, pulling from new muscle

Josh: As a child, you ate deeply of the earth.

and untarnished determination, until the nurse's amazement turned to exasperation.

Once when you were seven months old and we were visiting Grandma Sylvia in Texas, Dad and I took you to the Gulf of Mexico in Galveston and set you on the sand twenty feet from the ragged surf. Like a baby sea turtle you scrambled for water. Curious, Dad and I watched, wondering how long it would take for you to start crawling back once you got wet. You entered the water full speed, a breaking wave showering you with spray. Undaunted, you crawled on. The rolling tide lapped up to your chin and wetted your wispy blond hair, but still you continued to crawl. As one wave completely washed over you, we both broke into a sprint. Dad swooped you up from the foamy murk and lifted you high. You came up beaming. When he set you on the damp sand, you scooped a large handful and bit into it like an apple. As a child, you ate deeply of the earth and all it had to offer. You still do. Now, at twenty, you have grown long and lanky with your reachings into the world.

Jonny, you came into the world seventeen years ago, unresistant as pudding, your face covered by a membrane, lace-veined as a violet, which the doctor had to peel away. The veil of second sight, some call it—insight you use as pragmatically as a paring knife to pit circumstance to the core.

When you were eleven months old, I took you to the pediatrician for your checkup. She placed you on the examining table to measure you (commenting on the broadness of your chest) and checked your ears, eyes, throat and reflexes. Most babies on their back are like overturned bugs, limbs flailing about trying to gain purchase on something sturdier than air. But you lay placid and relaxed, staring at her as she poked and palpated.

Discomfited by your odd behavior, and speculating about a possible hearing deficiency, she clapped her hands loudly just above your face. To her bewilderment, you maintained steady, unblinking eye contact and startled not at all. To allay her concern, I assured her that you listened intently, heard well and already had a small wellspring of words. You were unflappable, both then and now. Perhaps it's because you inherited the Axelrood muscular build and are sinewed by deep roots that bind you to people, place and a firmly anchored perspective.

Jonny: You inherited the Axelrood muscular build.

Jonny, you left behind a pair of well-worn sneakers, each one big enough for a newborn's bed.

There were so many things I meant to tell you both, wanted you to know. So many secret places I wanted to explore with you in the same way we found the uncharted cinote in the Yucatán, by word of mouth and many false starts into the jungle. But the intended spirit journeys were muscled out by trips to the playground, to the dentist, to soccer games. By learning to tie your shoes, whistle, do square roots, drive a car right off the map of our everyday life together.

I wanted to be shaman. Instead, I became drill sergeant. Eavesdropping on your growing years, I hear my traffic signal repetitions: "Stop. Go. Wait."

How could I help you study for history, memorize revolutions and rulers, inventions and economies, and not tell you about your own history? Not tell you why Grandma, to barricade against famine, saves everything: magazines, tiddles of yarn, salt packets from airline meals, a year's worth of egg cartons in her garage, locked into cardboard Lego stacks.

How could I instruct you about organic foods, about fats and food groups, and not share the special hunger of my soul and what feeds it? Not tell you what nourished the souls of all your relatives at the end of whose umbilical you now sky-dance?

Partly because you are both so wise in your own way, partly because you are young and free-floating in the world with all its possibilities, you may not feel the need right now to know your spiritual legacy—the hate you will experience, and the love, because you are Jewish; the strength you can draw from the marrow of your own bones when there is nothing else left; the satisfaction of an explosive sneeze because there is no fear of being heard.

But when your family dies taking with them their untold story, part of your very being is lost in the terra incognita of the never-to-be-discovered.

Some parents don't speak because their story is unspeakable. They have never told (not even their own children) that they were in Auschwitz, in Buchenwald. They have never compared tattoos with their grandchildren.

Almost every day some activity catches at my gut—as I ferret cord with a safety pin through the tunnel of a pair of sweatpants, or grip handrails lest the stairs disappear (as they do in my dreams)—and I try to remember. Did I tell them, did I tell them? Little things, forgotten. Big things, omitted. Things that, because I didn't know how to tell you, my hands and eyes tried to word.

So, late as it is, I'll try to relay some of this root knowledge essential as all those drill-sergeant rules of safety and well-being. More essential, really.

Nightly, along with books about fantastical adventures, I should have been telling you your story. Shown you how fractaled patterns bloom infinitely outward, as well as infinitely inward. But the problem is that I don't understand it myself. I'm still trying to figure it out.

So. Where to begin?

I guess it makes as much sense to begin with this morning as anywhere. After all, no matter how far-flung we are from each other, we still look at the same sun.

Chapter 1

Slowly, by degrees, I wake. From under the comforter, I slip out of Dad's embrace, leaving those inscrutable coordinates of sleep that splay from the point where all space begins, where all time meets. Where dreams unite people, out of sequence, out of place.

My feet burn as they touch the floor, unable to cipher for a moment whether it is heat or cold that shocks them. Some mornings I'm so perforated with fear, so gape-mouthed with awe at the undertaking of another day, that in order to reach the window, I pass over live coals, over ice undercut with chasm.

Outside, the colorless scrim between sleep and waking begins to lift, and from the haze, apparitions of the familiar seep into shape: a density in the distance that will darken into Mount Nittany; the spreading red maple by the road; the shed; the forty-foot blue spruce that, when you were three, Josh, you climbed bough by bough to the top as I gardened. "Joshy," I called. "Come down, you are too high."

"No, I'm not," you replied. "I'm more than that. I'm three high, four high, five high."

In the widening, granular light, forms are so blurry, a moth wouldn't be able to find a leaf or twig substantial enough to grasp. Cries of a cardinal pickax their bright metal into the morning, the crimson flight across the yard as startling as blood outside the body.

I tiptoe downstairs in an erratic pattern to avoid the maze of creaks that plague old wood. Not that there is anybody to wake now. Both of you are gone and Dad sleeps heavily. But just as new habits are hard to form because we forget to use them, old habits perpetuate because we forget to stop. I discovered that along with the true meaning of "body of knowledge" when our beloved dog, Chita, died. My head knew she was gone, but it was well over a month before I could get out of bed without wide-stepping over her place on the floor. The body holds on to what it knows far longer than the brain.

In the kitchen, I pour some coffee and sip in the silence. Sweet and milky, it rolls down my throat opening round as an O. Astonished, I begin the day just as if I had never before tasted the elixir of that first swallow of coffee, never felt the exquisite lick of morning light warming my chilled skin, never experienced the sweet pressure of chair rungs holding up my body like outside bones. All this newness despite the fact that I am surrounded by visible history. Over in the corner, holding the spider plant, is the junior chair that held each of you long before you learned that the world turns on its own without your spinning. You learned quickly, though. When you were six, Josh, you came into the kitchen while I was scrambling eggs and said, "Mommy, did you know that if you woke up in the middle of the night, the kitchen would be where the living room is?"

"How does that happen?" I asked.

"Because," you replied, "every day the world turns the whole way round."

Perhaps that's the reason I can never find my way to where I'm supposed to be—the green center that eludes the chomp of chaos. Sometimes when I'm driving along the highway, the road hums under the tires as they revolve over traffic strips grooved like a phonograph record. Was it *National Geographic* that postulated the theory?—re-creating the voices and sounds of ancient artisans by placing a phonograph needle on a round clay pot and following the ridges made by the potter's tool. And what sound might have been captured? Would humming be heard, some heart, unleashed from time and flesh, spinning out from an ancient potter's wheel? Or instead, hoarse hawkings, a rusty guffaw?

Some stories from the past may be as speculative as sound twisted from the carapace of a vanished potter. But not yours, Jonny and Josh. Not this story. Not when you can look at a photograph of your aunt Lisa taken in her early forties and see a bandage on her left ankle. I remember the stories told to me about Aunt Lisa and her sore that never healed. The ulcer appeared in 1919 (many years before the photo) as she walked from village to village searching for her two-year-old daughter who was lost as they fled the pogroms.

Everywhere I look, Josh and Jon, your history is chaptered; the lopsided basket that holds pencils, the clay pinch pot that holds paper clips, woodshop projects of towel rods, napkin holders and spice racks. And especially the pine trestle table that bears your early hieroglyphs incised right through paper into its soft wood—alphabets and numbers, stick figures, rainbows, suns as big as teacups, plus marks and equal signs proving that the world adds up.

This is not remembered history that the mind can cobble into its own versions, it is as real and present as the dust that accumulates on it. It belongs to the everyday—a past you can pull up to the table or use to flavor today's soup. A past that echoes in the particulars of daily life.

Life may be created in the bedroom, but it is in the kitchen that it is sustained.

Still barefoot, I head to the basement, taking from the sink as I go the metal bowl heaped with kitchen scraps. Rinds, shells, piths, seeds. Lacking sturdier digestive systems, we feed mostly on the fleshy middle of things, just as we receive the heart of each day from the cracked bones of our ancestors.

I tug the cord to the basement light. The bulb flickers, then goes black. I feel my way down the uneven cellar steps, sponging in the dank air. It's not a smell I relish, but an animal quickening compels me to scent it deeply. A cold sweat of groundwater exudes from the pores of the cellar stones; water that has filtered through centuries of the living and dead, now bound in this subterranean space. I shove my feet into a pair of mud-encrusted clogs and clop out to the garden.

The morning is mistless and defined now. No fog to muffle clarity of thought. Rising beyond the woods on the opposite side of the creek, the green hills are pricked with the first red of the season, and slow rust gnaws at the leafy edges of the garden.

I unlatch the gate to the chicken yard and fling the scraps in a wide arc into a flurry of squawks, then go to gather eggs. In the dusty, slatted light of the chicken house, I reach into a nesting box, sliding my hand under the spread breast feathers of a golden brown banty—like the one that, when you were five, Josh, you dubbed Judy Morning Daylight. Groping gently, my hand curves around a warm oval, and I grasp the age-old paradox in my palm.

Chicken or egg, I wonder? The answer, I suppose, lies in the egg that lies within the chicken that is in the egg. Like this story. Where does it begin? Which birth? Which mother? How can I speak your story, Josh and Jonny, without a long history of mothers nudging these words into a laundry list of things that must not be forgotten?

After collecting the eggs, I stride to the garden.

Cold circles of damp seep through my sweatpants as I kneel on the ground to grip the sinewed stems of a beet. This, I imagine, is the way it would feel to throttle someone's scrawny neck. Shivers tunnel down my spine at the thought. In the maelstrom of daily fears—illness, accidents, random violence—it's odd to feel my own body turn predator.

I tug.

The stem resists. Again I yank, and from deep inside, from that place where energy turbines into action, where chromosomes and coffee swirl together with daily need and lunatic dreams, memory churns into motion, fueled by a list of helping verbs (like the one you, Jonny, brought home from fourth grade)—

am
is
was
have
had
do
did
might
must
would
should
can
will
be
being
been

Surging from that place that compels us to scratch our nose or journey to the moon, I hear a voice.

"Shalom, Joann," Great-grandmother Chana says. "Such a nice garden you've planted. Your first beets?"

Startled, I feel my blood jet through my veins and pound against my eardrums. "Yes," I whisper. "Detroit reds. Fifty-nine days."

"You hoed," Chana says. "Got blisters."

Blisters, I remember. Watery, aching pillows for the seeds to dream and grow lush upon.

"The first green," says Chana. "So hard to tell leaf from weed. And now time for pulling—easy for a strong woman like you. Pull, Joann. Pull."

"The root's long," I say.

"Long? Of course it's long. It reaches all the way to my gratchkeh in Tetiev. It begins here, here in Die Goldeneh Medina, your golden country, where people drink sun from a cup. And then, you know what happens? Along the way it sips from your buried relatives: Uncle Berney, Uncle Itzzy, Lisa and her baby, Aunt Roochel . . ."

Finally, I wrestle the beet from the earth. It lies, dark red, in my throbbing palm.

"Eat, child, eat," Chana urges. "So you shouldn't be hungry."

I pull more beets and carry them to the house, the long roots trailing.

Overhead, a flock of geese honk. I stand looking upward, head flung back, to watch them inscribe the frail blue. The sky, vast as a whale's belly, swallows me whole. What can I say that makes any sense? "Dear God, what did I do to deserve this?" Joy or sorrow, the answer is always the same. Nothing. Everything.

The geese surge on, receding in the distance, pulled through ancient starlight to the place where they belong. What gold, I think: to know unquestioningly where you belong, what it is you are supposed to be doing. And then, when the time comes, to be called from some deep knowing to the next place.

Slowly, I climb back up the dark cellar steps and begin to scrub the beets in the sink. Chana, compact, sprightly, her keen blue eyes sparking like flint, follows with the surety of seasons. It is hard to imagine so small a woman, a woman who has borne and raised seven children, still so energized, still so vibrant, each cheek a rose.

"Gramma Chana, tell me," I ask, "how do you know?"

"Know what, child?"

"What mothers are supposed to know?"

"Know? Achhh! What is there to know? You hoe your gratchkeh, the bread you knead until it feels just so, when comes the baby, you push. For this you need to know? Your heart, do you tell it to beat? Your breath, do you say 'now in, now out'? So what's all this 'know'?"

What other mothers know, Gramma. That certainty, secret as monthly blood. My mother-in-law, for instance. In 1934, when she and her husband and their five sons lived in upstate New York, she strained maggots from the kitchen pump with a flour sack, kept a ready umbrella for the leaking outhouse and managed the scant family finances from a cigar box. Her hands, so impregnated with soap they cleansed by their very touch, were always patting globed cheeks, chubbed arms, round bottoms, as if she were pressing pie crust from a lump, stretched enough to fit the pie tin, sturdy enough to hold ample filling. She smoothed their rumpled hair like fresh bedsheets, and each of her sons grew up knowing he was loved best.

I flick the last residue of dirt from the bristles of the vegetable brush, rinse the beets and swish the muddy water down the drain.

"I keep thinking there is this special key, Gramma, similar to the ones for a house or a car that children are given as they come of age—and that this special key opens a secret place, a sanctuary or a stash of treasure. The trouble is, I can't even find the door."

Chana picks up a small paring knife and begins to cut the

stems and roots off the cleaned beets, chopping with precision. "Keys, doors . . . huchhh! This door you look for, can it keep out a bullet? Will it say to the flames of a fire, go back, not here?

"Questions, questions. What means this, what means that? Look at the men with their watery eyes, Joann. They squint at their books for so many years, they squint out all the color from their eyes. They clutch their foreheads with their hands ready to snatch the live thing inside that gnaws to get out. But always, there are more questions."

"So what am I supposed to do, Gramma?"

"Do? Make the soup. That's what you do."

I heft the great soup pot off the shelf—my grandpa Morris's borscht pot—a huge iron cauldron big enough to bathe babies in (as I did you, Josh and Jonny) or feed, along with good black bread, a dozen or more lusty appetites.

Maybe I should stop for a minute, Josh and Jonny, and outline the Axelroods' family tree. I need the clarity even if you don't. I am no more adept at figuring out great-aunts, uncles by marriage or cousins twice removed than I am at finding my way across town.

Starting as far back as I know, we begin with Shimin's father, Yosef (your great-great-great-grandfather, Josh and Jonny), who was the source of the original family fortune before it was lost during the pogroms. Sometime in the early 1800s, in the southwestern area of Russia known as the Ukraine, there was a feudal lord called Graf Petotsky who controlled vast areas of land near Daaschiv, in the state of Kiev. One of Graf Petotsky's enterprises was the manufacture of vodka, which required the use of copper kettles. Yosef was an expert in the fabrication and repair of copperware. When Graf Petotsky decided to establish an estate along with a vodka distillery in the town of Daaschiv, he naturally chose Yosef to supervise the construction and maintenance of the copper distillation kettles. At that particular time, Yosef was living in the village of Yosterbinitz, about seven miles from Daaschiv. When Yosef accepted the job with Graf Petotsky, he had to commute fourteen miles a day by horse and buggy. Petotsky, observing Yosef's travel problem and wanting to retain his efficient services, made an outright gift to Yosef of a large tract of land. The gift was made with the provision that Yosef and his family settle there, just outside the town of Daaschiv. Along with the land, Petotsky allowed Yosef to take from the nearby forest all the lumber needed to fence the land and to construct a house. The tract that Petotsky staked out for him was so vast that Yosef was reluctant to expend the enormous labor to cut the lumber for the fence. Under the cover of night, he pulled up the boundary that Petotsky had staked out and replaced it to enclose a much smaller area; after all, how much land was needed for a single family?

Today it's hard to imagine many people saying, "I want less." When did this "all you can eat" mentality start? This insanity of stuffing ourselves and our lives to the bursting? More property, bigger houses, belts with extra notches. Where are these values from? Certainly not the Native Americans, who, in their reverence for nature, believed ownership of land was as absurd as ownership of the wind.

Remember when you were five, Josh, and gave me a

"gold" necklace—lavender yarn strung with raw carrot circles? "Count!" you urged. A bit puzzled, I counted. "1, 2, 3, 4, 5, 6, 7, 8, 9, 10, 11, 12, 13, 14."

"It's just like the one I heard about on the radio," you said, "a fourteen-carrot gold necklace."

Is our penchant for dazzle the reason we assess gold at three hundred dollars an ounce and carrots at four cents? Why do rocks have more worth than roots? Because one remains while the other rots? Or one is finite while the other can seed itself again and again? By that same yardstick, people become debris while the fillings in their teeth are mined and hoarded. Precious stones do have value—they saved our family's life on more than one occasion. Yet if you offer a starving person collateral or sustenance, the economy of the body prevails. Be vigilant, Josh and Jonny. High-gloss notions of success will urge you where to stake out the territory of your life. But if, like Yosef, you find the boundaries need to be reset, go quietly as he did and bring them into balance. For in the end, we spend the currency of our days on what we hold precious.

Of his downsized plot of land, Yosef gave one half to his niece Sarah as a wedding present and one half of the remainder to his brother. In the year 1900, when the Axelroods moved from Daaschiv to Tetiev in western Russia, the quarter part that Yosef had retained was sold for 3,500 rubles. At that time in Russia, 3,500 rubles could command goods and services equivalent in value to about $700,000 in the United States today.

Yosef had built his house on this land, which was about

two miles from the center of Daaschiv, in a tiny dorf called Pahlyova. Here, your great-great-grandfather Shimin was born, grew to manhood and married the beautiful Chana. There were only six Jewish families in Pahlyova; the Axelroods, the Benders (cousins to the Axelroods), three branches of the Schullmans (also cousins), and in later years, the family of Shimin's oldest son Ben.

As nearly as can be estimated without proper records, which burned in the pogroms, Shimin Axelrood and his wife Chana were born in the early 1860s, about the time of the Civil War in America.

In their shtetl—the self-contained Jewish village within Pahlyova—the diminutive Chana bore a total of ten children, seven of whom survived birth and early childhood. Fortified by a shot or two of vodka, Shimin, a quiet-spoken man, drummed his fingers on the heavy wooden table and prayed for the health of his wife and the safe delivery of his children, while Chana labored in the bedroom, hands clenched around the iron rungs of the bed, and pushed out in succession:

Barel (Ben)—born in 1882, died in 1940 in Chicago

Moishe (Morris)—born in 1884, died in 1954 in Chicago (your great-grandfather, Josh and Jonny, father of Grandma Sylvia)

Malech (Mike)—born in 1891, died in 1975 in California

Yitzchak (Isaac, changed to Irving in America, known as Itzzy)—born in 1894, died in 1947 in Chicago

Roochel (Rachel)—born in 1898, killed in Russia during the pogrom of 1919

Baruch (Berney)—born in 1898, died in 1968 in
Chicago
Rachmil (Robert)—born in 1900, died in 1970 in
Chicago

All six of the Axelrood brothers had blue eyes: the blue of del-
phinium, the blue of an immense unbroken sky, the cartogra-
pher's blue of the twelve seas that fist into the vast perimeter of
Russia. And all the brothers were unusually strong, especially
for Jewish males, whose usual occupations of sedentary study
and retail business exercised brain more than biceps.

Jewish boys and men were regularly taunted, not only because of their religion but also because of their comparative
weakness and unwillingness to fight. With Uncle Ben, that was
a big mistake. At five foot seven, 180 pounds, he was no giant.
But in the Axelrood foundry business, Ben was accustomed to
pouring kettles of molten iron weighing fifteen "pid"—about
six hundred pounds.

Once in Tetiev, he was walking along minding his own
business when two local peasants fell in behind him and began
calling him a dirty Jew. Ben tried to ignore them, which they
interpreted as fear. Finally, when he reached the limit of his
endurance, Ben turned and decked first one, then the other.
When the first one arose, he was again slammed down. After
that, the locals didn't mess with Ben.

My strain in hauling Grandpa Morris's soup pot off the
shelf would have been a feather's worth of effort for Uncle
Ben. With the pot now squarely resting on the stove, I follow
Gramma Chana's advice in the face of unanswered questions
and proceed to "make the soup."

Into the soup stock, made the night before, I put the scrubbed beets, their cut roots bleeding. To this I add a head of coarsely chopped cabbage, two large onions, a handful of lima beans, lots of garlic (six or seven cloves), several tablespoons of lemon juice and salt.

"The bones," Gramma Chana says. "You forget the bones. Bones and stew meat."

"We're vegetarian, Gramma. We don't eat beef."

"Achh, no matter. Beets are flesh enough. But don't forget sugar," Chana says. "Without a pinch of sugar, it's not right. Like life. You got to have the sweet with the bitter. Tears and laughter. Like the drop of honey put on a Jewish child's first book so that learning from the first taste is sweet," she says. Then she evanesces as easily as steam.

"Pinch of sugar," I repeat, reaching into the sugar bowl. There, among the shifting crystals, memory brushes against three crouched bodies, their faces upturned in fear. They are your great-great-grandfather Shimin, his handsome face now creased and gentle under a full white beard; Uncle Ben, the oldest son, massive muscles protruding as he hunches in the confined space; and Aaron, Rachel's husband and Shimin's son-in-law.

"Uncle Ben?" I say, taken aback.

"Shhh," Uncle Ben hisses. He whispers so quietly, I have to bend closer.

"Last night, the first pogrom erupts in Tetiev. It is a beautiful September evening. We all gather at my house for the bris [circumcision] of my new son, when the Cossacks gallop into town shooting and looting. They break in on us. We all flee in different directions. Papa Shimin, Aaron and I run

five miles to the sugar factory and climb into this crystalliz-
ing vat.

"Here," says Uncle Ben, sliding some sugar into my hand.
"Please, find my wife Lisa, my little Anna and our baby son.
Make sure they are safe."

"Uncle Ben, they're on the roof of your house," I want to
say. But how can I? Lisa is so young and beautiful. Like a prayer
shawl, her every cell was knit with the highest good. The
Cossacks try to rape her, but by showing them her new baby,
she convinces them she would not be suitable. Lisa is safe,
Uncle Ben, I want to say, little Anna and your son, too. If only
Lisa, who put such value on education and artistic beauty,
could see herself—a rooftop Chagall in the night sky, ringed
by a corona of stars.

But your sister, Rachel, who was on the roof with them, is
hit by a stray bullet. Rachel, Aaron's wife, Shimin and Chana's
only daughter. All night, from the roof, Lisa pleads for help. In
the morning Rachel dies. When it seems that the gangs are
gone, Uncle Ben, you and the rest of the family will struggle
back to Tetiev. Then you will find out. You see the slow convoy
of wagons carrying more than two hundred bodies to the
cemetery. You bury Rachel in the common grave, where each
family heaps its dead together. Years later, remembering your
only sister, your heart still aches with the weight of all two
hundred. You'll know soon enough.

I put the lid back on the sugar bowl and sprinkle the sugar
into the steaming pot. Some of it sticks to my clammy hand,
and I lick it off. Sweet . . . and bitter.

When I turn around, Gramma Chana is back, standing by
the sink.

Rachel: Shimin and Chana's only daughter

"Now," she says, her forceful, lilting voice unperturbed, "bring it to a simmer so it cooks nice and slow the rest of the day."

I peer into the pot watching the bubbles, a fragrant sauna bathing my face. My nostrils tingle at the sharp prick of onions.

"Gramma Chana," I say, "why do you give me recipes but not blue eyes? I always wanted blue eyes like you. Like Grampa Morris and my mother, Sylvia." My eyes are brownish. "Isshy" brown.

"Your eyes are blue too, child. It's just they have a layer of dirt over them. Dirt and manure."

"Dirt?"

"From your uncle Berney when he had to bury himself. Early in the fall of 1918, that same night of the bris, your uncles Berney, Robert and Itzzy run to the home of a local priest, where they cover themselves with dirt underneath a tree. Three grown men listening like roots to the boots of the roving gangs that pass over them."

"And the manure?"

"Achhh. Manure. That's another story. But look at your oldest son, Joann. Joshua has blue eyes."

"Yes. Like his father."

"No, not his father. Not genes. Generations. With time, the sight finally clears. But the heart . . . achh . . . it takes more than time for the heart."

"But my brother George has blue eyes, and he's older."

"So? You think life's fair? Everybody gets their own struggles. Some come from before them. Some are new. Like leftover soup. To what's left in the pot, you add a little something extra. Your struggle, Joann, is always to see clearly. What's there. What's hidden."

"And what's to come, Gramma."

"Oy! What's to come? Huhh! Such joys. Such sorrows. With so much to carry every day—pails of potatoes, babies, aching bones—who could bear a load like that besides?"

"I'm small like you, though, Gramma."

"Small is good. Better to hide. Less to feed. A shorter fuse to the flame inside."

I go to pour another cup of coffee, turn around, and she is gone. I sit down at the kitchen table facing the pot's throaty rumble.

Sipping slowly while thinking of Gramma Chana, I hear Dad coming down the stairs. He brings with him, as usual, an energy that bulges the air around him, an anticipation, the way cooking food proclaims its presence beyond its actual space.

We sit down to breakfast. Not the breakfast that Dad's father partook of every morning of his adult life: Wheaties, orange juice, two eggs sunny-side up, buttered toast and black cof-fee—forty-seven years of unrelenting order; through the birth of five sons and the death of two wives; an edible recita-tion as exacting as the Lutheran catechism he preached. Dad and I eat a simpler but equally unswerving breakfast—fruit and cereal, hot or cold depending on the season.

Why, I wonder, do we create and cling to these little tem-plates of ritual? Is it an attempt to pattern certainty into our lives? Or is the need for ritual silted in our bones, guiding our actions as surely as the migration of swallows? And can we ever hope to understand the immense intricacies that coalesce into a single action, a single response? Will we ever be able to map the geography of mind and spirit, blood and bone, in the same way we do earth? A simple three-line address pinpoints a single speck among millions, yet we scratch our heads in befuddlement over the most basic human behaviors. Why one baby cries and another looks on with curiosity at the approach of a stranger. Why some people succumb and others overcome. Who can explain without suppositions, footnotes and the hedging of bets in the babble of the day?

Questions, questions.

We finish breakfast, and Dad hugs me.

"I don't think I'll ever be able to get it together before it starts coming apart," I say.

"Before what comes apart?" he asks.

"Mind. Body. All those saddlebags of worry collapsing into a heap before I can figure it out."

"Worry about what?"

"Everything. The sorry state of the world, what I'm supposed to be doing about it. But mostly the kids. Are they eating enough? Do they feed others? Are they healthy? Are they safe? Will we end up like your dad, eating canned peaches in a nursing home, wearing diapers, not knowing our own children?"

Dad massages my slumped shoulders, pulling them backward and up the way you would rebend an overburdened wire hanger. He kisses the top of my head and leaves for work.

My shoulders slump back. (Remember, children, to this day, Grandma Sylvia keeps loose jewels in her safety deposit box so that, in case we are invaded by enemies, we can sew them into the hems of our clothing.) Emergency collateral. Carats for carrots. Or safe passage. It weighs down every skirt and shirt, every dress and coat I've ever worn or will wear. Even when I try to straighten up, I'm tugged by their undertow. They are your unspoken heirloom. I stitch them into the seams of your life as I pack gloves and socks, water and candles and granola bars into a survival bag for you as you drive cross-country. Tuck packets of cocoa and dried soup instead of Styrofoam into the boxes of clothes and books that we mail to you; stuff the toes of your shoes with bottles of vitamins.

What you perceive as "mother's quirkiness" is really just part of the long root you have spooned from your soup bowls for so many years.

Grandma Sylvia

Chapter 2

WORM

KNOWLEDGE

A BREEZE BLOWS IN THROUGH the open kitchen window from the farm next door and clobbers me with the smell of manure. Though not entirely pleasant, for me the smell of dung is always strangely intermingled with hope. Whether I'm shoveling out the chicken coop or hunched over the toilet bowl scrubbing, I think, what better promise than excrement that life, despite everything, goes on?

Draining the last trickle of coffee from my mug, I think how odd it is to discover at fifty that geography is everything. Ironic, especially for me, since I would be hard put to name the various seas or to locate Jakarta on a map. Even to point west from where I sit (though we've lived for years in this house), I must first go through elaborate gesticulations to figure out north, south and east—a signing of the cross.

Yet here I am in Pennsylvania, standing on this particular longitude and latitude of interconnected lives, dazed and teetering from an uprooted beet. This unseen geography holds me to everyday life along with who knows what? Sweat? Love? Breakfast? Dreams? And it catches up my breath to see what lies underground. For me, much of what is mounded under that ground is fear. Fear of suffocation. A fear that hobbles thoughts, actions, choices. Something learned early and deep—a metaphor of blood.

I often wonder if it is fear of being buried like Uncle Berney or because I was stillborn. My head, firmly clamped by steel, was pulled from the tenacious grip of Grandma Sylvia's womb after two days of contractions. Mauve and silent, strangling in cord, I received my first feel of hands. Hands that demanded life. The doctor's hands on the soles of my feet, my buttocks, insisting with repeated slaps . . . live! *Live!* Someone's mouth on mine, suctioning, blowing me up like a balloon. Then baths. Hot, cold, hot, cold. Commanded to live, I did, filled from the first moment with someone else's breath.

"Joann is such a good baby," beamed my mother, Sylvia. "She only wakes to eat and already she is smiling," Mother stroked my dented head to memorize its bumpy topography. She knew that years ago, it was by this same braille of bones that our cousin Anna was recognized and reclaimed. Little Anna who, you remember, on the night of the first pogrom huddled with her mother Lisa, her baby brother (still bleeding from the bris) and her dying aunt Rachel on the roof of their house.

Suddenly, the kitchen door bursts open, shrieking on its hinges. I clutch my coffee cup, braced. Stunned by the muscular handsome man who fills the doorway, I notice his uneven gait as he stomps the mud from his boots. "Uncle Berney?" I rasp.

"That's right," says Uncle Berney, next-to-youngest of

Shimin and Chana's six sons, his blue eyes smoldering with anxiety and an abiding wry humor.

I expect him to remove his black Russian cap and hang it on a coat peg near the door, but he doesn't. Of course. It is the working man's yarmulke, covering the head as a sign of respect in the presence of God.

He limps in, the result of a hip dislocation. In 1916, just before his eighteenth birthday (your age, Jonny), Uncle Berney, like all Russian males of age, was required by law to report to the local draft board at a specified time and place. World War I had started in 1914.

Remember, children, for a Jew life in the Russian army was either sure death or a living hell. Because of inbred hatred toward Jews, insults were commonplace and the Russian officers could beat enlisted men at will. In addition to the physical hardships and brutal hostility, the crude, roistering life of the Russian peasant-soldier was anathema to Jewish family life, with its emphasis on ritual and learning. To avoid military service when they came of age, two of Berney's brothers, Ben and your great-grandfather Morris, *zay hoben gamacht ein oyehr*— "they made themselves an ear."

Not for the faint-hearted, this excruciating and dangerous procedure was accomplished by pouring carbolic acid directly into the ear canal until it burned through and perforated the eardrum. Berney's other brother, Irving, endured a self-inflicted hernia. Robert was still too young and Mike went to America. But when it came his time to avoid conscription, Berney went to a quack doctor who dislocated his hip.

"Anna," Uncle Berney says breathlessly. "Ben's little Anna . . . have you seen her?" I motion him to sit down.

Beads of sweat run down his furry cheeks, sweat collects in dark ovals under the arms of his tunic-style shirt.

"Since early spring," he says, "people whisper that the peasants of Tetiev and the nearby villages are organizing another large-scale pogrom."

Pogroms, derived from the verb meaning "to break or smash" and "to conquer," were organized attacks by groups of gentiles against Jews, long sanctioned by the czarist government, involving systematic arson, looting, rape, beatings, torture and murder. Life usually returned to an uneasy peace afterward, with Jews and gentiles going their separate ways. But the pogroms took on an even more virulent nature after the 1917 Bolshevik Revolution. Berney is talking about the pogrom in the spring of 1919.

"Tonight," he continues, "I am just getting ready to leave the foundry when someone brings in his gun for repair. I overhear the man casually remark that there will be bloodshed this evening. Imagine, bringing his gun for us to fix! I leave immediately to tell everyone. Since Ben's house is closest, I stop there first. The pogrom starts even as I tell of it, so I am forced to stay. All of us, Ben, his wife Lisa, their two-year-old daughter Anna, their six-month-old baby boy and some neighbors quickly go to the secret room in the cellar when we hear the gunfire."

"Secret room?" I ask, getting up to pour him a mug of steaming black coffee.

"Do you have to be bitten by the flea of God more than once to learn how to scratch?"

"Sugar?" I ask, but he is already reaching into the pocket of his tunic and removing two lumps.

Noticing my surprise, he pats his pocket and says, "Always, I carry sugar. You never know when there will be an uprising. Some to keep the children quiet. Some to stop a cough. Remember the first pogrom early last fall?" he asks. "The night of the bris? Ben and Lisa's son already marked for God by the mohel's swift knife, the Shabbas candles dripping, the wine half-drunk when the Cossacks break in. That was the night our Roochel, hit by a bullet, weeps silent red tears. Robert, Itzzy and I fled to the priest's garden and buried ourselves under the tree until the next night. True to the Sabbath, we spent the day resting. It was then we knew we must prepare a secret room."

I pour another mug of coffee for Uncle Berney and put out a plate of bagels and some cream cheese, a bowl of cottage cheese and a basket of fruit.

"Would you like some eggs?" I ask.

"Eggs? No. No, thank you," he says, sniffing the air.

"Soup," I say. "Borscht. Just started."

"Borscht? Yahh," he says heartily. "Some borscht."

"But it's not done," I say.

"Neither am I," he answers with a lusty laugh. "But I may be soon. Better have it now."

"Really, Uncle Berney," I protest, "the soup's not ready. I could get you some—"

"Soup." He says it with finality. "Worries go down better with soup."

I stir the contents of the pot, hoping to hasten the barely cooked vegetables, then fill a brown crockery bowl and place it before him with a spoon.

He bows his head, and I hear the resonant murmur of the

familiar Hebrew words: "*Boruch ato Adonoy Elohenu Melech Ho olom hamotsi lechem min ho orets.* Blessed be Thou, O Lord, our God, Ruler of the world, who causes the earth to yield food for all." He raises his head, dips some soup, and closing his eyes, sips audibly, swallows and smacks his lips. When he opens his eyes, they are welling with tears.

"Yes," I answer softly. "Your mother Chana's recipe. Without the bones."

"Mother," he says, visibly shaken. "Such a beautiful woman, God rest her soul. That a wagon ride could cause such a cheerful, good-hearted woman to go to her death is unthinkable. But now, with Roochel her only daughter dead and her children hunted like animals, that too is unthinkable. Do you know one thing death spares us?"

"What?" I ask.

"The sorrow that follows," he says.

"Where was the secret room, Uncle Berney?"

"Below the house. After the first pogrom, from the day we buried my sister Roochel, God rest her soul, my brother Ben begins to build it in the cellar. Right under a toilet, he makes a passageway. You could raise the toilet, go partway down the passage, replace the toilet from underneath and continue down into the secret room. He digs another passage under a false wall that separates the cellar from the secret room. In it we put food, water, candles, tools and a wheelbarrow to use in emergencies."

"Today, when you came from the foundry, was that the first time the secret room was used?"

"No," he says, combing his fingers through his thick, light brown hair. "Only a few months ago, in December, General

Denikin's troops were passing through, and they stop in Tetiev to procure more supplies in the strange manner of war. Instead of being recompensed, we whose goods are taken have to pay—with our blood, our bodies, our burnt houses. But who has a choice? No choice *is* a choice.

"Everyone, all the Axelroods and our neighbors the Landas, hurry into the cellar to hide, hoping the raiders take what they want and leave. Everyone except me."

"Where were you, Uncle Berney?"

"Me. Achhh. That's another story."

"Weren't you there?"

"I was there all right. Upstairs in bed, too sick to move."

"You must have been dying to stay upstairs at such a time," I say.

Nodding, Berney takes a chunk of bread and sops up several mouthfuls of soup with it. "Typhus," he says, swallowing. "A 105-degree fever. Some Denikintsehs come crashing in. They make a terrible racket smashing what they cannot take. Then they find me. One screams, 'Communist, give me your money!'

" 'I'm no Communist,' I say. 'I have no money. Only typhus fever, which I will gladly give you if you come closer.' So he beats me over the head with a club," Berney says, pulling his hair back off his forehead to reveal an ugly scar.

"Even from the basement, Papa hears my screams. He runs upstairs to plead for my life. They seize Papa. They put a rope around his neck, loop it over the rafters and hoist him off his feet. Last thing I remember before passing out is Papa dangling from the rope."

"Shimin died?"

"Life as he knew it died," Berney continues, holding out his bowl for refilling. "Cancer of the throat took the rest of him a few years later. Rachmil, little Robert, only fifteen years old, saves him. He breaks free from the family, who try to hold him back in the cellar, and gun in hand rushes upstairs and cuts the rope around Papa's throat in time.

"By then, the butchers are gone. Again, we bury our dead and wash away the rubble with tears."

"But today?" I ask. "Weren't you hiding again in the secret room today?"

"Yes. Today we were all safely hidden. A cold cellar grows damper with sweat of so many bodies. But nevertheless we begin to feel warmer and warmer. We all shvitz like crazy. And then we smell smoke. They set fire to the house. What could we do? We had to leave. So Ben and I, using the tools we had for just such an emergency, break through the wall leading to the outside.

"We all flee in different directions. Less chance to be seen. More chance for at least some to survive. Ben carries little Anna, Lisa the baby. Instinctively, though each by a different route, we all head to Yossip's house. Yossip Bursuk, a lanky, hard-working gentile with sad eyes, for years works in our foundry. Years before, Yossip lost his wife and two children to an outbreak of the fever. He is a close friend to our family, and we know he can be trusted. What we do not know is that, when the pogroms begin, he anticipates our need and cuts a hole in his granary floor that he has built about a foot and a half aboveground as a barrier from rats.

"So this time I run with my hobbledy-hop hip past a bridge where I see hooligans. I change direction. I run and hide, run and hide, until, exhausted, I finally reach Yossip's house. Even though anyone caught harboring a Jew is killed on the spot, Yossip immediately takes me to the hole in the barn floor. I lower myself down flat on my back, and he replaces the boards two inches above my nose and covers them with straw. There is no rolling over. But as the saying goes, a man who lies on the ground cannot fall. For twenty-eight days, I stay there. Many times the Cossacks' boots stomp right over me.

"Yossip, when he approaches, to let me know it's him, he always whistles a Russian drinking song. As I lie there, this has two influences on me. One, my throat remembers how thirsty it is, and two, my bladder remembers how full it is. Whether to harness his horses, milk the cow or, praise God, let me out for a few minutes, Yossip whistles.

"With the Cossacks, it is not melody that signals their coming, but rumble and thud. Here I am, stretched out flat, unable to scratch an itch or brush the crawling things that tickle my scalp, march across my face, tunnel in my ears, find their way up my trousers and into my shirt. Sometimes I am able with a quick jerk to shake them off, but many times I must simply endure.

"So often in life we think that we are master of our own universe just because we can create day and night by opening and closing our eyes. But believe me, in a position like mine, you find out that we all have our path through life, and many times we must share the path with unlikely travelers. Lying thus, my backbone also serves as an extra ear pressed to the ground. The distant gallop of horses vibrates my bones. Rumble becomes the clompety-clomp of hooves, closer and closer until my whole body is a drum and I cannot tell which are the horses and which my pounding heart. The Cossacks shout and stomp, first here, then there. And it is then I begin my disappearing act. For this I have a method.

"First I take away all my thoughts: like a broom, I sweep clean my head. Then my body, like some big bear in the winter, I put to sleep. Everything I make slow down—my beating heart, my breath. I say to myself, 'Berney, go somewhere else. Back three years before our beloved mother, Chana, died; before the death of our sister, Roochel. Go back to the Sabbath table with the family washed and dressed in their Sabbath best. Watch Mother, like a glowing bride with the lace veil over her head, light the candles in their polished silver candlesticks and say the blessing. Watch as she beckons with her hands for the joy and peace of Sabbath to enter into our home and hearts. Watch Papa, sitting at the head of the table, bless the bread and the wine. Leave these sorry bones of yours, Berney, and go somewhere else.' So you see, I am both there and not there at the same time. You understand?"

"Yes, Uncle Berney," I say, barely able to speak.

We have names for it now—guided journey, meditation, daydream. When yearning, pain, stress or fear pushes us to the brink, we can go "somewhere else." I escape to an island cloistered in my dreams. Lush, uninhabited, lucid blue water lapping onto white sand. And raspberries. Always raspberries, their blood-red juice like prayer beads on my tongue. Beneath palm fronds outstretched in benediction, I lie swaying in a hammock, my bones full of light, and pray. Pray for today. Pray to be guided by yesterday, because affliction, whether past or present, brands deep into the brain. That's why to miners, the underground is veined with possibility and the threat of cave-ins, and to me, it is laced with roots, soft-bodied worms and relatives.

"Like a dead man," Uncle Berney continues, "my body lies without a blink. Nearby, a shout. The Cossacks enter the barn, slamming open the door, shoving aside the horses to make sure no one crouches in the stall, thrusting their swords into rustling stacks of hay, into sacks of feed. Voices closer, farther away, then right on top of me. Boots kick up chaff and dust that winnows down through the cracks and chokes the narrow air below. And without warning, my body snaps back as I feel a big sneeze running up and down inside my nose like stinging ants. I can't raise my hands to pinch it closed. I can only hold my breath and squeeze until my eyeballs pop." Thinking of ants, Berney scratches his long brown beard. "Let me tell you, in a position such as mine, one has a great deal of time to think and pray. I wonder if all coffins echo so."

"And Ben and little Anna?" I ask.

"Anna. Anna," Berney mouths, the sound sucked from his voice. "Ben clutches his small daughter in his iron grip and runs in a different direction past the cemetery. There he is attacked by a group of eight men with guns. They seize him. Ben knows that he is recognized when they do not ask him to pronounce the Russian word *kookeroozeh,* meaning corn. This Russian test word would earn you an instant bullet during the pogroms because Jews, speaking mainly Yiddish, roll their *r.* Ben, as the rest of our family, has practiced much, but here there is no chance. One of the eight men raises a gun to Ben's head ready to shoot, when out of the crowd a man steps forward and shouts, 'Don't shoot, he's a *good* Jew.'" Berney sighs. "One never knows."

"Knows what?" I ask, the coffee I had drunk corroding my stomach like acid.

"Knows what a bit of kindness can patch. Shoes, hatred . . ."

The fine hairs on my neck prickle. "I don't understand."

"Ben, some years before, owns a carriage factory. Every so often, he is asked for the leftover trimmings of leather. The peasants use this leather for patching their shoes. Once Ben has a whole bushelful to give. It is to the man who now speaks on his behalf, saying that he is a 'good Jew.'

"The man shoves Ben and Anna. 'That way,' he says, pointing out a safe route. 'Hurry, before someone changes their mind.' Exhausted, Ben makes it as far as Andreyan's house, which is closer than Yossip's. But even though Andreyan also works for the Axelroods and is a loyal friend, the situation is so dangerous that he begs Ben to leave. Bullets can be heard close by. The roving gangs search every house for Jews, shooting them and any gentile who hides them. Anna clings to her father with terror and begins to cry.

"Inside the house, smelling of onions, Andreyan's wife stands off in the corner, her six children, eyes big with fear, hovering in back of her, beside her, clutching her apron.

" 'The little one?' Ben pleads. 'With so many of your own, who will notice?'

" 'Agreed,' says Andreyan. 'Until it is calm again.'

" 'And if Lisa and I are killed,' Ben whispers urgently, 'and none remains of my family, will you take care of her?'

" 'Yes,' Andreyan solemnly swears, binding his life to

Anna's in the way so many enter the strange matrimonies of war. 'And if we cannot keep her, we will place her with a good family.' Anna is pulled from Ben, soothed with sugar and the bosomy embrace of Andreyan's wife, so much like her mother's.

"Ben leaves that night with a weight in his heart far heavier than the one his arms leave behind. He walks by dark and rests by day. On the third night, after walking a distance of sixty miles, he reaches safety and Belaya Tserkov, which means White Church.

"When Ben arrives at Belaya Tserkov, he is overjoyed to find our father Shimin and two of our brothers, Robert and Irving.

" 'News of Lisa? Of Berney?' they ask each other. But there is none. So many killed, so many families separated, so much suffering and chaos. Before bread, before soup, at rising, before sleep, they close their eyes and pray. 'All-wise ruler of the destinies of man, I cry from the depths of my sorrow.'

"After several days, they decide that they must leave Belaya Tserkov and go to Kiev. They hope greater resources in the big city can aid in locating Lisa and me—if we still live. And Ben, though it is not safe yet, is anxious to return to Tetiev for Anna. With the whereabouts of his wife and his baby son unknown, and bereft of his little Anna, Ben lies on the floor of one of the Jewish families, who offers shelter and prays with heavy words that drag him into sleep: 'Days of anguish and nights of weeping hast Thou meted out to me.' "

"So, Uncle Berney, while you're lying underneath Yossip's granary floor, what happened to Lisa and her baby?"

"Coming toward Yossip's, she finds a barn and buries herself in the straw with her baby son. This is no easy task as Lisa is well rounded and, compared to most Jewish women, fairly tall—about five foot six. Two days she stays without food and water listening to the shooting, galloping horses and scream-ing—sometimes it is near, sometimes farther away.

"Rats scuttle everywhere. Bugs and flies crawl over them day and night. The baby cries. She suckles him. Again and again he cries. She tries to clean his dirty linen, wiping his chafed bottom with straw and then ripping pieces of petticoat from beneath her skirt to pad his soiled diaper. From her head she takes her kerchief—a married woman must show her hair to no one but her husband—and wraps her son to comfort him and protect him from insects.

" 'Shayne yingele, beautiful baby,' she whispers to him as she tucks him into a snug little package like a blintz. Her stomach gurgles as she thinks of the thin pancakes filled with a taste like heaven and tender as the skin on her baby's bot-tom."

"My mother, Sylvia, has a secret recipe for blintzes like that," I say to Uncle Berney, by way of a moment's escape from pogroms and bullets and rats.

"With cheese?" he asks.

"With cheese. She beats three eggs foamy. Then, through a sieve, she mixes in two and a half tablespoons of cornstarch and two tablespoons of flour. To this, one cup of water is added and left to rest about thirty minutes. She always uses a special heavy skillet, about six to eight inches, which she but-ters between each crepe with a brush. She cooks only one side and then turns it onto a towel and puts on a generous dollop of filling made from ricotta or cottage cheese (about a pound), mixed with four ounces of cream cheese, three eggs (but only two of the whites), a pinch of salt, cinnamon and sugar to taste, and a handful of soft raisins. Then she rolls it, neatly tucking in the ends. We would eat as she cooked them one by one, spooning on top sour cream and strawberry preserves or chunky applesauce. Pure bliss, I remember."

"Yah," says Uncle Berney. "Somewhere I'm sure it is written. Somewhere there must be a *mitzvah,* a commandment, that 'Thou shalt share such secrets as thy mother's recipe.' Life has so many hungers. So many mouths clamor to be fed—the mind, the stomach, the soul, the heart, the pocket. When you find a food that feeds several mouths at once, it is a special blessing in the eyes of God.

"So . . ." he says, pinching the skin between his eyebrows and taking a heavy breath. "While Lisa thinks of blintzes, her baby's cries dwindle to whimpers. She suckles him almost without stop, but by the second day, her milk parches from fear and lack of water. He nurses and cries, each time more weakly. Toward nightfall, the baby's whimpers stop, and when she shifts his floppy little body, she sees he is not breathing. Frantically, she pats his back, then his cheek, but he does not move. She unwraps his body and kneads his chest and stomach as if it were bread that she could make to rise. Massages his legs, slaps the tiny soles of his feet, strokes his arms and curls his fingers to grasp her own, but they drop open. Slowly, with greatest care, she rewraps him, bending close to whisper in his ear, 'shayne yingele, shayne yingele.' Kissing his forehead, she wraps the blanket over his face and sits rocking him as she waits for dusk.

"Scraping out a shallow grave with her hands, Lisa buries

him near the barn and prays while her ears listen for bullets and horses. 'The Lord giveth, the Lord taketh away, blessed be the name of the Lord . . .'

"Her parched tongue sticks as she mouths the words. Her breasts are shriveled. And in her eyes, there is a terrible sting as they shed salty, waterless tears. Then she makes her way through the dark to Yossip's. Without telling her that I am there, Yossip takes her up to the attic and hides her behind piles of straw. The rats rustle as she dozes. She startles, thinking that her baby stirs. She prays and weeps: tearless, silent and itching."

"Why didn't Yossip at least give her the comfort of knowing that you were there, Uncle Berney?"

"Yossip knows if they find one of us, they will ask probing questions before they kill us. Those anti-Bolshevik Cossacks have their ways. If we know of each other, a little look, a small word might slip from one of the wounds. But if we don't know, what can slip out but blood?

"So as often as possible, Yossip lets us out one at a time. Sometimes only every couple of days because of the danger. I relieve myself, wash, eat a little bread, some groats, some cabbage, squint in the bright light (even the stars burn my eyes like cinders) and try to bear the burden of my upright bones. Then I return to my narrow study to lie down and think.

"I think about things done and not yet done. Here I am, twenty-one years old, still unmarried. My oldest brother, Ben, knows marriage, children. My second-oldest brother, Morris, has a wife and children also. But most of all he has safety. Twelve years ago, before all the fighting begins, when he is in his early twenties, he leaves for America to avoid

After a year, Morris (left) sends for Mike.

conscription. There he learns modern foundry techniques. After a year, Morris sends for Mike, my third-oldest brother, the one with the noodle for how things work.

"Funny how things work out. Mike is only sixteen. Because Mike is so young, our papa, Shimin, sends one of his trusted employees with him as a traveling companion. For a while, this traveling companion stays in America with Mike, and then he returns to Tetiev with considerable savings, enough to let him live comfortably. The name of this traveling companion? Yossip Bursuk.

"In the dark, on my back, I think about things and I pray. 'O Lord, in the gloom, I look to Thee for light.' Strange how in life you yearn for more time to study and reflect and pray. And in hiding you ache for the feel of an ax handle, a woman, the soft earth beneath each stride. So much fills that little space beneath the boards that sometimes I can barely breathe. You know how sound travels underground?"

"Yes," I say, handing Uncle Berney an orange and a sharp knife.

"So do thoughts. And prayers. And roots. It becomes very crowded under this floor of Yossip's.

"Then, lo and behold, on the twenty-eighth day, Yossip brings me out into the house. The shutters are pulled. There in the slatted light I see an apparition, a dusty half-ghost woman. It is Lisa. Both of us, weak from immobility, quiver like jelly in each other's arms. Yossip says that the butchers have left the area. It is still not safe for us to travel in the open because the anti-Bolsheviks are still fighting the Bolsheviks. Everyone suspects everyone else of being a traitor, but Yossip has a plan.

"It will look to everyone just as if I am going to fertilize my fields, Yossip assures us. Lisa and I, we lie down in the wagon holding hands. Yossip gives to each of us a hollow reed the same color as the straw that litters the fertilizer. This we have to hold in our mouths between our teeth so that we can suck the air. Then, layer after layer, Yossip covers us with manure.

" 'Something will grow from this,' I tell Lisa, squeezing her hand as Yossip hurls the damp black clumps over our feet and legs, then our bodies. It grows heavy, heavier. It couldn't weigh more if the horse were on top of us instead of pulling us. We take our last look at the sky, which at this moment looks good enough to eat, and Yossip begins with his own hands to scoop manure over our heads and lay it gently over our faces.

"Under ordinary circumstances, the smell of dung, almost plugging our nostrils, might make us sick. But during such times as these, we were already accustomed to the stench of fear. With practice, almost anything can be learned.

"Now I know what it feels like to be a wagon. Every rumble and bump, every grind of the wheels rattles our bones. Stifled from lack of air, baking in the sun under the reeking dung, Lisa later tells me how thoughts of dirt weigh down on her.

"She thinks about this mucky business called life. How her hours are filled with scouring and sweeping and scraping and scrubbing. How this pile of dung is not so different from the soilings of her own family; the feces, urine, mucus, sweat. How even when we are washed and wiped, we foul the world with unclean thoughts, with wasteful purpose. How in the chain of mess-makers, we now find ourselves at the bottom, along with the worms and beetles and fleas and lice. She almost laughs at the thought, except she fears losing the reed between her teeth.

"But bumping along, there was one big difference from the lying down for twenty-eight days on Yossip's barn floor—we were moving forward.

"Fifteen hours later, we are in Belaya Tserkov. Stinking, wobbly, free, we part from Yossip, no words possible to express our gratitude. I tell him how to find the place where Shimin buried some gold and jewels at the beginning of the pogroms. But I don't know if he ever found them.

"What I do know is, shortly after we arrive in Belaya Tserkov, Yossip, this good man, not so strong as some, not so smart as others, nor overly good-looking; this ordinary man who without a mutter swallows the dose of the day and goes on in extraordinary ways—this man to whom we owe our life—is arrested by the Bolshevik police.

"Some of the Jews who fled from Tetiev have organized a resistance unit. They are helped by the Bolshevik soldiers, who grudgingly include Jews in their new social order because they need their expertise in business and trade. Together they go back to Tetiev to liberate the remaining Jews who still hide in various cellars and attics. The rest of the Jewish population of Tetiev, over four thousand, has been decimated. Now it is the local peasants pleading for mercy, each one saying he had nothing to do with the atrocities."

I shake my head in disbelief at Uncle Berney's words.

"What's to be surprised about?" he says. "The seasons, they change. Trees one day are green, the next bare. Pockets full this day, empty the next. The dark beard grows gray. So who can tell when the hunter will become the hunted?"

"What happened after Yossip was arrested?" I ask, bringing a dampened dish towel. Berney mops the juice from his beard and mouth, from his hands, and sets it next to the orange rind peeled in a single spiral, which sits on his plate like a hollow globe, slightly askew.

"Ahh, Yossip. Someone recognizes Yossip as one of the residents of Tetiev and notifies the Bolshevik police. When Lisa and I hear this news, we rush to the court to plead for his life.

"To the police I say, 'This man, Yossip Bursuk, has saved our lives. For over a month he hides and takes care of us.'

" 'With no thought of the terrible risk for himself,' Lisa interjects.

" 'This is true,' I say, as I continue our plea for Yossip. 'And with no thought of receiving anything in return.'

"Lisa begins to weep. 'Because we must hide, we can do nothing. Yossip Bursuk takes care of us like children, feeds us, keeps us safe. For us, he must do everything,' she says, knocking with her fist on her hollow breast.

"The police listen and grant clemency. We embrace Yossip. We fumble with words, but what can be said? Lisa and I each have two lives now—one given to us by God, the other by Yossip. We are struck tongueless. Funny thing, words. We study words, we pray words, we cobble together words to make stories, but for some things, in the face of horror, in the face of the holy, there are no words. In the dark days under the floor of Yossip's barn, I discover this silence; a beyond-words silence so quiet it roars; a silence that holds no words and all words at the same time; a silence that knows all things, understands all things.

"Again we try to express our gratitude to Yossip, but in times like this, there is only one possible language—New Life—a covenant of breath and blood where every action we make is repayment for this debt, this gift, this miracle. In this new language, silence swells the mouth, and it is the heart that must speak.

"The police escort Yossip out of town, saving him from almost certain death at the hands of the vengeful survivors of the Tetiev massacre."

Who can tell when the hunter becomes the hunted? I guess that's part of what stumps me, Josh and Jonny—how to discern quicksilver from the immutable. They both shape-shift. Like you. When you were born, it took your whole hand, warm and moist as new bread, to grasp one of my fingers. Now your hand enfolds mine as you tower above me.

Eyes are not trustworthy either. Many evenings, I go sit at the edge of the creek and gaze into the mirrored reflections. I see fish feeding in sun-speckled trees; shadow birds winging through the weedy creek bottom.

Swimming upstream, two mallards seem to glide without effort. But hidden from sight, their webbed feet muscle powerfully. As the sun sets, dusk drains them of emerald iridescence. Soon the colorless forms lose outline, become unbound matter. With no palpable clue of flesh and feathers right before me, how can I ever hope to grasp the unseeable, the unknowable, the eternal?

It's getting cold. The water of the creek rushes by. I stare into the dark, mole-blind, and wonder how to instill in my children enough spiritual resilience for the journey; for the frequent jostle and stench of the wagon ride. Is it too late? Without the steadfast rituals of my relatives, I am bereft of a starting place. Maybe that's why geography baffles me—I have no locus. I lack the rites that wolf-mark the territory of our brief life: the blessing of wine, the lighting of candles, the prayers for every occasion. Is this what comes of a mixed marriage? Dad, the goy, the Lutheran preacher's kid who wondered, at age five, if little African children who never heard of Jesus could get to Heaven, and me, the unsaved daughter, wanted our children to be more than just Jewtherans.

We wanted your spirits unfettered by dogma; unbound moving matter; to give you a faith that saved the unchosen as well as the chosen; in which sacraments were anchored in the moment; where kneeling to scrub the toilet was baptism enough, and cutting vegetables branded you for God as surely as circumcision.

We joined hands before meals and sat in silence. Dad and I felt the holy instant, the blessings of family and food and the opportunity to add to the balance of good. But did you? Or were you, as it sometimes seemed, merely giggling at each other's burps, deciding which you would eat first, your potatoes or your beets?

Without words, did you learn how to pray? In rejecting the rote, in considering everything sacred, did we make nothing sacred? In discarding Hallmark holidays for everyday words of love and support, did you receive the message that our passage through life is without milestones? That the wagon ride ends not in destination but another journey?

As newborns, you wrapped your tiny hand around my finger, an innate reflex to hold on to something. Is this the same reflex that causes us to create graspable images of where we have come from and where we are going?—mezuzahs, medicine bags, chain-dangled symbols, certificates, souvenirs, photo albums and letters to our sons?

I envy those with unflinching faith; those who take scraps and shreds and, with fine, even-handed stitches, quilt them into whole cloth. The world brims with so much beauty, full of fleet miracle, of arch and leap and furl. But it also swarms with destruction and despair. The duality leaves me mired in confusion. I long for simple possibility. An apple seed. A grain of sand in an oyster. A caterpillar. I want light and flight and daily transformation.

Taking a tin of butter cookies from the pantry, I ask Uncle Berney, "Did you and Lisa find out that your family had gone to Kiev?"

"You think *network* is a new word? News spreads faster than the cholera among our people. One yenta hobbling on her sore bunions goes to buy cabbage at the market. 'Did you know,' she says, 'that so and so, mother of so and so, left on Friday at such and such an hour, and can be contacted through the Blooms?' She stops to talk to the tinker. 'Did you hear that the Brodsky baby has the croup?' She passes her neighbor on the stairs. 'Have you heard Samuel Levine knows of work at the factory?' Each person tells two others. Before the yenta can reach her home and open her string bag to remove her cabbage, the whole town knows. With such a system of mouths, who needs this telephone of yours?"

"So," I ask hopefully, "you found out that everyone else had gone to Kiev?"

"Yes. We found out where my father Shimin and brothers Robert, Irving and Ben had gone. But not before we met up with Chova."

"Who is Chova?"

"Chova," repeats Uncle Berney, smoothing his scruffy beard. "Out of the ground we scoop holes and tunnels. Like the moles. Like worms. Like men, hiding. Then we cover them up. Build over them foundations. And this we call firm? Huhh! Under our feet is anything but solid. Except when you have to dig postholes," he adds with a throaty chuckle. "Yah, we think we are protected. Bricks, beams, walls, foundations. But under there," he says, stomping the floor with his boot for emphasis, "nothing but a few clumps of dirt and holes. You flip a ruble and take your chance. Sometimes you step firm. Other times you slip through."

Uncle Berney, weary from flight, lulled by warmth and a full stomach, lapses into a silent meditative nodding.

"And Chova?" I ask again.

"Imagine," he says, with an abrupt and audible intake of air, "a young girl of eighteen, still in the green years of her life. She works, she dreams of a husband and family. One day, when Yossip lifts the floorboards of the barn and I fumble upright trying to remember what feet are supposed to do, Yossip whispers what has happened.

"You see," Uncle Berney continues, "many of the Jews, over two thousand, run to the synagogues when the pogrom begins. But the army sets them on fire, burning them and all the people inside to the ground. Many others are massacred.

Others flee Tetiev. But there remain a few hundred—women, children—imprisoned for weeks in a barn. The roving gangs rape them, abuse them. But now a local priest and a handful of good-minded people come to the town square and ring the church bell. They bring together all the other residents of Tetiev. They appeal to them for common decency. As an act of Christian charity, they set free this raggle-taggle group from the barn. They give them some bread to divide, and herd them out of town like a bunch of cattle.

"Andreyan, who still hides Ben and Lisa's little Anna among his own children, sees these stragglers as they flee. Every hour of the day and night, he lives with the terrible risk of keeping Anna. As he watches, he sees in this group Chova. Though she is but a hollow shadow of the young maiden he remembers, he knows Chova to be the daughter of another worker in the Axelrood foundry. Quickly, he seeks her out and explains how it is that Anna comes to be with him. Then he presses Anna's hand into hers. Chova promises to look after Anna. To bring her to safety. All day the group struggles on. At dusk they arrive at the village of Cherepin, some seven miles from Tetiev. They begin to search for a place to rest when they hear shots. So what could they do but run?

"Chova arrives in Belaya Tserkov only a few days after Yossip's fertile journey brings us there. Chova tells us how she is forced to leave little Anneleh in Cherepin.

" 'She is too small to go fast. Anna is safer there.' Her voice is flat, emaciated with despair and exhaustion.

"Lisa pleads with Chova for information, a little wisp of something that will help locate little Anna. But Chova's eyes are mute. Terror corrugates them like the inside of a cabbage, fear folded upon fear. So. What can we do? It is not safe to go back to Cherepin. And we have now the news that my papa Shimin and my brothers Ben, Robert and Itzzy are in Kiev. They have no idea we are still alive. Lisa and I leave for Kiev. Ucch, such a reunion! Who says the dead can't return?"

I watch unspeakable joy illumine Uncle Berney's face, and a heavy stone feels as if it will rip through my heart. I remember when I told Chana that I struggled to see what was to come and she said, "With so much to carry every day, who could bear a load like that besides?" She was right. I can't bear it. But I can't tell Uncle Berney either. Let him digest his half-cooked borscht and the memory of his reunited family. Let him at least have that. Later, years later, he will find out what happened when Chova panicked at the gunshots and ran.

Anna wasn't the only child left in Cherepin. Many others were left behind in the dark. Who knows whether Chova really thought that Anna would be safer in Cherepin? Who knows anything when the unthinkable happens, when the whole world turns into rabbits and wolves? This much is sure. Little Anna was worn out after the grueling trek. She was a little more than two, still a toddler, and unable to run very fast. And Chova, after being held captive in the barn for nearly a month, starved and raped, was stripped of everything but horror and the raw instinct for survival.

I bring the coffeepot over to pour Uncle Berney another cup. "It's time I get back to Ben and Lisa," he says, taking the coffeepot and setting it on the table. "In Kiev, they wait for me for news of Anneleh. One must not depend on miracles." He gathers my small, birdlike hands in his strong, rough, capacious ones.

"Already?" I ask.

"Life is like unleavened bread," he says. "In order to live, we must eat whether the bread is risen or not. Even during the Sabbath, when the braided challah sits upon the table yeasty and fragrant, we know that time stops only for this one little moment. The week races by in work and trials. The years race by. But on the Sabbath, everything stops. The mother kindles the Shabbas candles. Silently she beckons their light into her heart and asks the blessing, 'Oh Lord, Thou art our Light. In Thy Name we kindle these Sabbath lights. May they bring into our home the beauty of truth and the radiance of love's understanding. Amen.' Before the bread is broken, a blessing is said. A blessing is said for the wine, symbol of joy."

Uncle Berney releases my hands and plucks two Red Flame grapes from the basket of fruit. He places one in my hand and holds the other one up between his thumb and forefinger.

"See. Like unleavened bread, here is wine."

"Wine?" I say, staring at the grape.

"This little world holds everything. Past. Present. Future. From it you can grow a vine, eat, drink, remember." He raises the grape high into the air.

"*L'chaiyim,* to life!" Then he pops the grape into his mouth, closing his eyes to savor it.

I do the same. *"L'chaiyim!"* We embrace tightly and he leaves. The door shuts, and I sit down at the table, shivering in the cold draft.

I take a deep breath and let it out slowly.

Eighteen-year-old Chova. Two-year-old Anna. Burning houses, bullets. Josh and Jonny, do you ever remember us hugging you so hard and so long that you felt as if you couldn't breathe, as if it would never end? That's the hug of parents holding their child for all the parents in the world whose arms go empty. Parents whose children have been stolen from them by war, starvation, hatred, drugs, disease, despair. It is an embrace born out of guilt and gratitude that our child is here, though we are no more deserving. It is a fierce attempt to ring you with talisman and benediction.

To think of losing either of you is inconceivable, a profanation of all that is natural and holy. Water would change to stone. Stone to quicksand. I know that eventually all children are carried away into the world's tide and seethe.

But not like Anna, or all the other Annas in the world's unnatural history. This kind of history erases all boundaries. And when there are no boundaries, you cannot cross over or be held back. Everything bleeds into everything else. Nothing is solid or contained, it's all atoms, frenzied and fibrillating. Walls waver like objects at night when shapes expand and contract as if they are breathing. Floors undulate. There is no constancy, nothing is held fast. Even God moves by shimmer and shadow.

Lisa

Chapter 3

THE SEARCH

BEN TRIES TO REASON with Lisa. "It's only three weeks we are in Kiev. All is still bullets and burnings."

"Chova says my little Anneleh is in Cherepin. Cherepin is where I go," Lisa insists.

The family begs her to wait until it's safer. "*Bistu meshugge? Are you crazy?*" they ask.

But she cannot be restrained. "Could I keep running, even to save my own life, if out from my body had dropped my heart? Every minute, I hear her crying to me, '*Mameh, mameh, ich bin hungerik!* I'm so hungry. So cold.'"

There is no swaying Lisa's resolve. Ben, who pours vats filled with six hundred pounds of molten iron, is powerless. That night, he clutches Lisa in embrace.

Trembling, with the tips of his fingers, he strokes her dark hair, the graceful arch of her brows, her long lashes, fine straight nose, exquisite lips, the curving geography where he lives.

"A son lost, a sister killed, God rest their souls. A daughter disappeared. Please God, not a wife, too. A wife already delivered back to me from the dead. God protect you, my Lisa. May your journey not be in vain."

In the darkness, the air around them bends until they are enclosed in a black vault. Inside it, their short desperate breathing echoes.

Early next morning, Bessie Lifschitz, Lisa's mother, pulls her black shawl around her ample body, takes her wicker shopping basket and leaves their apartment in Kiev, which is near the Jewish market, the Evrayskaya. The reek of brine from the wet wood of the pickle barrels needles its way up Bessie's nostrils and brims out of her eyes as tears of worry for the dangerous journey that her daughter is about to make. Quickly, she dabs them away and buys two loaves of bread at the stand where a woman is selling rounds of rye and pumpernickel, heavy as cobblestones.

Barefoot girls kick at the sawdust by the stall of the meat vendor, who is as stocky as the pot roasts he sells and whose stained apron is tied, for lack of a waist, just below his chest. Small boys with yarmulkes, the fringe of their prayer shawls peeking out beneath their shabby dark suit jackets, poke at one another and peer at delicious-smelling cookies as they reluctantly trudge to a long day of study at the cheder. The fishmonger, long black sleeves rolled up to her elbows, calls out in a husky voice, "Carp! Perch! So fresh they leap into your cooking pot."

Mothers, intent as surgeons, instruct their daughters on the fine points of choosing the freshest cabbages, the tenderest greens. They inspect the stem end of apples, radishes and carrots for signs of bruising or rot, knowing from experience how much can be learned from examining the place of attachment. With one hand clutching her chest, Bessie can feel that place, a direct lifeline to Lisa, being cut. Clopping by, a horse-pulled cart passes, carrying books, pots and pans. The knife sharpener sits at the corner, spinning his whetstone and rasping blades to a keen edge.

Returning from the market, Bessie hands the basket to Lisa. "So you shouldn't have to eat trayf [unkosher food]," she tells her. "Here is bread, herring, cheese, hard-boiled eggs and pickled vegetables, a gift from the grocer who, when he heard of your trip, personally he fishes them out from the barrel. Also, some things to drink and a little something to make your journey sweet, God willing," she says, pointing to a sliced honey cake.

All gather for Lisa's leave-taking. Pauline, Berney's new wife, gives her an extra petticoat, still warm from her own body, to replace the ripped one that Lisa had used for diapers. "So at night you shouldn't be cold," she says, hugging her. From another comes some coins, produced like magic from scarce money, to tuck in the hidden pocket of her inside petticoat. From Shimin, a blessing. She is bathed by so many tears, she feels as if she has been purified for the Sabbath in the mikvah, the ritual bath.

But once gone, she is all purpose. No longer running and hiding, she is fierce; unswerving. She is traveling alone, a dangerous prospect even in the best of times: thirty-two, a beautiful, well-endowed woman, whom God Himself could not have stopped.

In Cherepin, she has just begun to ask when she meets up with the village watchman. He is a slew-footed, wiry little fellow who has a yeasty smell of beer and unwashed wool about him.

"About so high?" he asks. "Long dark braids?" Lisa nods.

"Big dark eyes like you?" he asks. Again Lisa nods, her breath starting to come in short spurts.

Lisa describes what Anna was wearing. "Yes, yes," he says to the description of the dress, the stockings, the shoes.

"One morning, several weeks ago, I was making my rounds. Out of the fog, I see a mound by the side of the road. It's early spring, the ground still frozen, too early even for the planting of onions. I approach and see children huddled together, motionless. Then I hear a muffled whimper. I begin to tunnel through the mass of bodies. Underneath, I find one small child, barely alive. It is the child you describe. I take the little one to my house, and my wife gives her sips of tea and warm gruel. Finally, the little one begins to look more alive than dead. She is so pretty, so smart. A few days later, a woman passes by and admires her. Says she would like such a child as this. And why not? Having such a pretty child gives one standing with her neighbors. But with a houseful of our own children to feed, we are glad to give this little one to her. She gives my wife a woolen shawl in return. Who this woman was or where she comes from, I could not tell you."

Lisa's heart stops beating with every new word. At the end of the watchman's tale, she is unable to speak. This man saved her child's life. Then he traded her for a shawl. She reels with gratitude and despair. Inside her, every cell cries out, She's alive, thank God she's alive! "Little Anneleh, Mameh will find you. Mameh's coming."

Ordinarily, for a Jewish mother, every aspect of a child's life is cause for anxiety. The hand-wringing worry that a mother daily bestows on her children is not only her way of showing her love, but also a protection. Worry is a Jewish mother's amulet against "God forbid, something bad should happen." And she has more worries than she has hairs on her head. "You shouldn't run so fast, you might fall. Be careful, you'll poke your eye out. Put on your muffler before you catch a cold. Eat one more little bite so you'll grow up to be strong. Study hard. You want to be smart, don't you?" For everything a child can think or do, there is an equivalent worry. And if there isn't, she'll think one up. (Sound familiar, Josh and Jonny?)

A mother will go hungry so her child can eat. She will sacrifice everything, sell her Sabbath pearls, eat less, to educate her child. And because a child is a mother's flesh and blood, it was not only her child that Lisa was searching for. Lisa, too, was lost.

Mother and child are connected by the cord that knits us all—the same network of veins in a leaf appears in butterfly wings, in bloodstones, in the eyelids of a sleeping child. Just as all roots wick water from the same ground as the amate, a fig tree whose flowers bloom within the walls of its thick-skinned fruit. There exists a single species of wasp that has the ability to penetrate the fig and lay its eggs. There the babies hatch, feast on the fruit and emerge to pollinate and reproduce, completing the life cycle of both wasp and tree.

Anna dwelled within Lisa's heart. Neither could survive without the other.

Starting in the vicinity of the watchman's house, Lisa knocks first on this door, then on that. At each house, she describes her child, begs for any clue, any recollection, any scrap of information that will lead her to Anna. She stops strangers, storekeepers, peddlers. The story of the weeping lady who lost a child becomes well known throughout the area. She walks endlessly. But at every stop, hope quickly dwindles to ash.

During this search Lisa develops an infection on her ankle. She pays it little heed. Besides, she reasons, the men put dried beans in their socks on Yom Kippur, the Day of Atonement, so that their discomfort is a constant reminder of God. At first her sore festers, then it becomes an open ulcer, oozing and throbbing with every step. "What use is a head if the legs can't carry it?" she moans.

Finally, after three weeks of searching without any further clue of the woman who bought Anna, Lisa turns back. After all, she has her other children to care for. From her first marriage to Abe Steinman, who died in 1912, she has Zena (Jean). Her beloved husband Ben has two children, Morris and Riva, from his first marriage to Enie, who also died in 1912 from complications of a miscarriage.

A mother's children are everything to her, and Lisa has to carry on despite a seeping ankle, and her stricken heart over the death of her baby son and the loss of little Anna. Frustrated, despondent and bone weary, Lisa prays herself back to Kiev.

"O God, if we learn more of Your love through struggle

and sorrow, why do I feel so abandoned? A hundred more dung heaps give me, but not this. Not little Anneleh. Give me strength to look through the shadows. Amen."

But in the midst of her prayerful murmurings, she frequently halts, frozen like an animal that hears a sound. Always, she hears the same thing over and over. "Mameh, mameh . . ." In the wailing of the wind, in the squeal of the peddler's cart, the cry of another woman's child. Each time her heart stops, vigilant, primed, hoping beyond hope. And each time, only by God's will does it begin to beat again. And then she prays still more.

I've struck something hard, Josh and Jonny. Something in our family's past, obdurate as bedrock, that refuses to be dug up. Forced to name it, I would call it faith. Faith in a God with ears. A God who seems reasonable enough to talk to. A God with hands who can reach out and part the sea, who can change walking sticks into serpents and burn bushes without consuming them. I long desperately for a faith of my fathers, of my mothers, a faith that can pray in the face of senseless death and unbearable misery. But the God of my understanding is some unnamable, unknowable mystery. Yes, I pray, I cry out, but not because I believe (as I yearn to) in answered prayers, in angels, in an omniscient and loving Mother/Father/Friend, but because I was born lop-headed, myopic, without breath and with too many worms churning inside not to believe.

As Kierkegaard says, "The supreme paradox of all thought is the attempt to discover something that thought cannot think."

. . .

When Lisa returns to Kiev, the family tries to comfort her.

"The world is more exacting than God Himself," her father says.

Her mother, Bessie, tries to treat Lisa's ailments, both the grief of her heart and the pus from her ankle. "Get it out before it poisons you." She treats Lisa with tea dosed with raspberry syrup, the first-ditch remedy of shtetl life, and with herb compresses.

To expel putrescence of mind and body, Lisa is prayed over and purged but all to no avail. Her ankle continues to ooze, her heart to weep. And as if she can bear still more, it is decided that the family will travel to America.

"Die Goldeneh Medina," Ben says. "Land of peace! No more pogroms, no more 'Jew, get out of here.' Opportunity for a new life, especially for the children."

"For all but Anneleh," says Lisa, saying what Ben cannot, as she tries to stretch her hope even further, to an alien land thousands of miles away. Her only comfort lies in her parents, Eefsay and Bessie, who will remain in Russia and continue the search.

Chapter 4

DIE GOLDENEH MEDINA

"IMMIGRANT. SUCH A LITTLE word for so much change," Uncle Ben, the oldest, says to his younger brother, Morris, your great-grandpa, Josh and Jonny. "So much struggle. A new life. A new land. So much to learn and to do that you forget the getting there. But the getting there, oiyee! That is a life in itself."

It is 1924 and they are in Chicago, sitting in the home of Morris, the second oldest, who came to America almost twenty years earlier. The door opens, and his nine-year-old Sylvia, whom everyone calls Sister, comes in bringing tea, which her mother has set on a tray.

She has the Axelrood blue eyes, and her beauty is marred only by a slight indentation on the tip of her nose caused by a sour cream jar flung by her older brother Bill, in one of his characteristic flares of temper.

"The little mama," Ben says. "Such dimples God only gives

Sylvia: Such dimples God only gives to His favorites.

to His favorites. All these little children waiting to be born, and God goes down the line and to just the special ones He puts His finger on their cheeks and says 'This one I like.' See. This is the mark. Right here and right here," says Ben, putting his finger into Sylvia's dimples and making her laugh.

"Oh, Uncle Ben. You are making that up."

"No. Is true, is true," he says, pinching her cheek.

"Uncle Ben, tell me the story of what happened when you left Tetiev."

"Again?" Ben says.

Sylvia nods emphatically, knowing that, though she has already heard the story many times, her uncle adds new tidbits each time. Uncle Ben pats his knee and Sylvia climbs onto his lap. Morris refills Ben's wineglass and shoves an after-dinner tray of nuts and dried fruits in his brother's direction. Ben takes a sip of wine, savors it a moment and begins.

"So many flee Russia in 1919. Not just pogroms to escape, but there is also war and lack of food. We decide to leave by way of Romania. But first we must travel by train to Komenske, a town just inside Russia, which faces the border of Romania. Simple, yes? Except there are no tickets to be had. Everybody's a refugee these days.

"Every day I go to the station. Every day the train is stuffed like sardines in a tin. To add to all the tsuris [troubles], your aunt Lisa's ankle swells to the size of a newborn's head."

"So? What did you do?" Sylvia asks, looking up into Ben's gentle face.

Ben sips the homemade wine and continues. "Even in the best of times, does a shelled egg leap into the mouth? Things are so bad, there is so little food, that with the heads of two herring, I bribe the conductor to let us ride. But not *in* the train, mind you. Still there is no room in the train. This is for passage on top of the train.

"There was Papa Shimin; Lisa, my wife, who is now thirty-two; and all our children—Rae (Riva) who is fifteen; Little Morrie who is thirteen; Jean who is nine; and as always, in our hearts, little Anneleh who is two. Also, there are our brothers Robert; Berney and his new wife, Pauline; Itzzy and his wife Netchah; Netchah's sister Geetle and her husband Nachman-Yosef; Boosie, Lisa's sister, and her husband Aaron. Fifteen of us. The whole two-herring family. Such an honor. For more than a hundred miles, we see the sights through the smoke of the locomotive and try not to fall."

"So you arrive. Then what?" asks Sylvia.

With his free hand, the other encircling Sylvia as she sits on his lap, Uncle Ben takes a dried apricot and nibbles on it thoughtfully before he goes on. "So then we have to get past the border guards and cross the Dniester River into Romania. This time, not so easy as two herrings. But we have a bit of luck. Itzzy's wife, Netchah—the beautiful Netchie, delicate as a porcelain doll—has an uncle in Romania whom she manages to contact. This uncle arranges for a Romanian guide to meet us in an isolated spot, a place with not too many guards.

"This happens as planned. The guide, in his black fur hat, leads Itzzy, Netchah, Geetle and her husband across the frozen river. So scared are they, they don't know if their hands get numb from cold or from holding each other so tight. They arrive on the other side safely. Immediately the guide goes back for another group, also trying to escape like us. This group

Itzzy, Netchah, and their baby daughter Faye (1922)

goes exactly the same way, but under them, the ice gives way and they all drown."

Morris shakes his head. "Man guides, God holds the reins."

Ben nods and takes a swallow of wine. His hand comes to rest on the massive, polished mahogany table, and for a moment, there is a heavy silence as if the swirled wood and Uncle Ben recognize that they are both strangers, cut off from their roots and transported to a strange land. As she looks up, Sylvia can see the curved hairs in Uncle Ben's nostrils quiver as he takes a deep breath through his nose, halfway between a snore and a sigh.

"For the rest of us it takes several months more. Proper contacts must be arranged even in improper times. There are border guards to bribe, local smugglers to pay. For this I use the jewels of my first wife Enie, God rest her soul. We have sewn these into secret pockets of our clothes. Still, there is no guarantee. Corruption is everywhere. Sometimes a border guard who has been paid handsomely will drown his passengers just to show the authorities that he does his job."

Morris shakes his head. "A man's worst enemy can't wish on him what life thinks up."

"Such is true," says Uncle Ben. "So the night arrives for the escape. First Papa Shimin and little brother Robert are ferried across the river. Then brother Berney and his wife Pauline. I cross with Lisa. The boatman dips the oars deep, so as not to splash. Then our daughter Jean and our son Morrie. All that remain are Boosie, her husband Aaron and our daughter Rae. But before the boatman can call the three from where they hide in the woods, the authorities catch him and beat him bloody. Aaron, Boosie and our daughter Rae flee back to Kiev.

Only later is Rae able to join us in Romania. Aaron and Boosie are so frightened by that night that they never again attempt to leave Russia."

Fear. Crossings. Decisions. Braced, we tread across boundaries that will separate us from those we love; pull us far from the place we call home. And too often, we do it in the dark, not knowing if we will arrive safely; not knowing if we will arrive at all; unable to predict how a flick of impulse in our brain that sinews us back through the woods to known terror, or across a frozen river to unknown terror, may shape the rest of our life and the lives of our children's children. I guess that's another comfort of faith. Trust. Knowledge there is a path when no path is visible.

Uncle Ben loosens his arm around Sylvia, whom he has clasped more tightly with each crossing of the rowboat.

"So," he continues, "now we want to go to the town of Kishinev, where there is a large settlement of Jews. From there we will be able to arrange our travel to America. But the problem is, we cannot gain entry into Kishinev."

"So then what happens?" asks Sylvia.

"So then it is that little brother Robert, who is now almost sixteen and has developed quite an eye for the women, proves he's a mensch. He meets a girl who is daughter to General Soloviev, a high officer of the local Romanian army. She thinks Robert is amusing and handsome, which, of course, he is. Sometimes too charming for his own good. And our Robert finds her friendly and, what shall I say? . . . willing." Uncle Ben throws a sly wink to Morris. "Through their friendship,

Robert has developed quite an eye for the women.

Robert obtains the passes we need to enter Kishinev." Ben takes another swallow of wine.

"Kishinev. Compared to conditions in Russia, Kishinev is a little piece of heaven on earth. Wine is cheap. Plenty of food. Believe me, in the Russia we left, only the eyes get enough to eat, never the belly. And the people in Romania, for the most part, they let each other alone. And what's more, jobs!"

"So that's when I send money and you come to America," Morris says, slapping the table with satisfaction.

"Not so fast, menschele," says Ben, using his nickname— little man—for Morris, who is shorter and less muscular than the other Axelroods. "You interrupt with the cart before the horse gets there."

"Der menschele!" snaps Morris. "Who do you think makes it possible for you to come to America? Who brings from Russia the whole family? Who, at age twenty-three, comes to America by himself in 1907 to escape the czar's army, where they take you even with holes in your ears so they can put holes through your body? Who comes to Cleveland in Ohio and works in a foundry? Who brings brother Mike to America a year after? Who goes to Montreal in Canada and works for the railroad company? Tell me, wise man, tell me who sends money home to Russia where you make in three weeks what I make in a day? Who moves to Chicago and works in the business of insurance and lumber? Next time you start with your 'Der menschele,' may you lose all your teeth but one, and may that one have a toothache!"

"Morris, Morris. You get too excited. Of course we remember. You bring us over. You help us all set up in business. You give a home to Papa and to brother Berney and Pauline. How could we ever forget?"

"Nu? So what are brothers for? It gives me pleasure. Finish already with this story of yours."

"So we wait in Kishinev for the necessary government papers, for the arrangements for travel, for money from you. Lisa and I, Jean and Morris, we all live in a room of a family by the name of Altman. The Altmans have five children of their own. When you are a refugee, you learn to know the word *refuge*—a word that makes its own *borucha,* its own blessing; a word that has a big heart and always another potato to add to the soup pot.

"Soon Berney, Irving, young Robert and I find work in a local foundry. Foundry work, this we know how to do. Hard work. This we know how to do, too. The owner offers to make partners of us if only we stay in Romania. Lisa begs for us to stay. And with good reason. Now, besides our three children, we also have Jackie, who was born to us in Kishinev in March of 1922. What's more, Lisa never stops with the questions about Anna. To everyone we meet, she asks, 'Have you seen . . . ? Do you know . . . ? Have you heard . . . ?' Letters and letters she writes to her mother, Bessie, in Russia.

"But even in Romania, there is no real freedom for a Jew, they must still live in a special section, the Jewish Pale. To make a living, a Jew may do this, but not that. A Jew may go here, but not there. Not like in Die Goldeneh Medina. For our children's sake, we come to America."

Freedom. Like love, beauty and God, it's one of those slippery fish words. It wiggles out of the confines of the very definitions that try to hold it firm. But just remember, Jonny and Josh, when you start quibbling about someone stepping on the toes of your freedom, how far beyond the pale you have traveled from your relatives.

How are most of us to comprehend a word so big as *freedom*? Probably not until we are burned out of our home, starving, on our knees clawing out a shallow grave for our baby. Even in America, this golden land, too many mothers have lived a similar horror, mothers whose names I will never know. We are largely nameless and faceless to each other. That is why we must remember Lisa, her name a yahrzeit flame in our hearts. Remember so we do not trivialize. Remember so we are vigilant. Remember because we are knit together, the free and the unfree, and a single snag can unravel us all. Remember because to forget is to lose a part of ourselves— who we were, whom we need to become.

Uncle Ben drinks some wine, offers Sylvia a sip and continues. "The first to leave for America are Robert and Papa Shimin. Robert works in the foundry only a short time before they sail for Canada in 1921. Yankel, Shimin's brother, already has come to Canada some twenty years before. He comes to meet them at the boat. But nowhere does Yankel see his brother Shimin. Nowhere does Shimin see Yankel. So Yankel returns home and Robert and Papa take a cab to Yankel's house, which is in Montreal. Such a happy reunion! That they didn't recognize each other at the boat is not so surprising. After all, for twenty years they have not laid eyes on each other. What surprises is that the gypsy had told it just this way."

"Gypsy?" Sylvia asks, her blue eyes wide with surprise at this new fact.

"Yah, just before Robert leaves Romania, he goes to see a gypsy. She takes his hand, and for a long time she looks. Then she tells him, 'When you reach your destination, your relatives will not recognize you, or you them. You will travel to their home, and then you will recognize each other. To reach your final destination, you will cross a border, but not legally. You will marry once, a relative, but this will not turn out well. You will marry again and become a rich man.' And so far, it happens just this way.

"Shimin and Robert stay with Yankel for two weeks. Then they take a rowboat across the border to New York State.

From there, they take a train to the City of New York, where they stay with brother Mike, and Sophie his wife and their children. For a month they stay before they come to you in Chicago."

"How does this gypsy person know?" Sylvia asks.

"You live long enough, you hear everything," Ben says, shrugging and stroking his shaven chin. The old country beards are long gone from the brothers.

"I told you already," Morris says, "I wanted that young Robert should go to medical school. In Russia, a Jew cannot become a doctor. But here in America, is a different story altogether. In America, you can become anything. I tell Robert, 'You go to school, I pay.' But he only goes to that preparatory school, Hoffman. Then back he goes to Sophie and Mike in New York and works engineering with the New York Rapid Transit. But this is not news. Tell Sister what happens next with you in Romania."

"May I have a piece of candy?" Sylvia says, eyeing the box of chocolates that Uncle Ben brought. "Please, Papa."

"Candy's no good for you," Morris says.

"Just because you don't like it, Papa . . ."

"It's not that he don't like," says Uncle Ben. "It's he ate enough for this life and the next. You never heard about your papa and the candy factory, Sister?"

"No."

"When your papa, Morris, first comes to this country, he gets a job in a candy factory. So to save money, he eats pieces of candy as they come from the conveyor belt. This way he saves money to bring over the rest of the family. For two years, he stays alive mostly by candy: fudge, solid milk chocolates, all kinds of bonbons—coconut creams, cherry cordials, caramels, nougats. That's how come, now, no more candy! Here, take some apricots. For you, some. And here is for your brother Bill.

"So . . . back now, to Romania," Ben continues. "Back to more train rides. But this time *in* the train. Not so many sights as in our two-herring ride, but neither do we have to worry about falling. Lisa and our four children, Rae, Morrie, Jean, and little Jackie who is more than a year old now, we all board the train in Kishinev and travel to Hungary, Czechoslovakia, Germany, Belgium. Finally we arrive in Antwerp.

"Such shpilkes the children have from the too long sitting. They make games with packing string. Over and over, they sing the same song. And the mother, she never stops. This one is hungry. That one needs a wiping of the nose. The other one needs to make a pee-pee. One's hot. One's cold. This one pinches that one. That one kicks the other. One sleeps. Another cries. And all of us think we go deaf with the clickety-clack of the train. Or that our heads will shake off from our bodies with the constant chuga-chug. Sometimes we don't know if we are going to Belgium or going meshugge. But even when finally there is a little moment's peace, when all the children finally sleep, Lisa does not rest. From her string bag stuffed with bread, cheese, a knife, a bottle of water, two handkerchiefs, a shawl, extra rags for her 'time' (as if the trip is not inconvenience enough), she gropes for a brown-paper-wrapped parcel. She unwraps the paper and removes a pen and paper to write to her mother Bessie, in Kiev, so that when the train stops, she can make a mailing. Never will my Lisa rest until our Anneleh is found, never. Until the day she dies, she will search. And when she dies, she will still search. This I know.

"Finally, we arrive in Antwerp and board the ship *Melita*. And next to Liverpool in England. And from there we sail to Canada. Our family stands at the railing of the boat, and as the people on the shore grow smaller and smaller, a lump grows in Lisa's throat so big she cannot swallow. The boat is big. More room than the cramped train for the children."

"That's good, isn't it, Uncle Ben?" says Sylvia.

"Not good. The waves take us up, down. Up. Down. Jean and Morrie grow green as cheese mold. Lisa's ankle makes such pain when she walks, she bites open her lip. Little Jackie, so happy to walk, toddles here, there, everywhere. One day he wanders near a pipe that makes steam. When the boat heaves, onto this pipe he grabs. Oy gevalt! Such a burn. Such screams. One side of his face, his neck, his arms, his chest. All the way down to his pupik, our Jackileh is red with blisters the size of boiled fish eyes.

"The doctor on the ship does what he can. The cook comes with cod oil. Day and night we take turns. Rae, Morrie and Jean, they sing to him; tell him stories to keep from his mind the pain. Lisa puts first one kind of schmear on him, then another. He is so full of grease, she calls him her little latke as she tends his burns.

" 'My little latke,' she says, 'my poor little fried latke. When we get to America, Mameh will make you lots and lots of latkes. So many latkes your tummy will grow round.'

" 'Oww, Mameh, oww!'

" 'Poor bubbelah, just a little more salve. We make you good as new. Do you know how Mameh makes latkes, bubbelah?'

" 'Noooo!' he cries.

" 'First Mameh peels three or four good potatoes, and she grates and grates. Then she takes the potato mush into her hands and squeezes out all the water. It drips out into the pan like this: sshht, ssshht, sshht,' she says as she gingerly strokes salve down his arms. 'Then Mameh grates some onion, about sooo much,' she says, making silver-dollar-sized dabs on his chest and stomach. 'Then two eggs, stirred round and round like this.'

" 'Ohh, it hurts, Mameh!' Jackie cries as she lightly swirls ointment onto his cheek.

" 'Into this, Mameh puts in two soupspoons of cracker crumbs. Then a little sprinkle of salt, a little sprinkle of pepper. And then Mameh takes spoons of batter and puts them into the frying pan with about this much fat,' she says, scooping up a gob of salve to warm in her palm, 'and fries them each side until they are crispy brown. And do you know what that makes, bubbelah?'

" 'Stop, Mameh, *please!*' Jackie cries.

" 'It makes beautiful little latkes, just like you. There, bubbelah. All finished,' she says, finding an unanointed place on his forehead to kiss. 'And you know what we put onto the top of the latkes before we eat them?' she says, wiping her hands and pulling over a dish. 'Applesauce.' She dips a little sauce onto the tip of a spoon. 'Just like this.'

" 'Not hungry,' Jackie says, exhausted.

" 'Try, bubbelah. Just a little. So you get better and can eat lots of latkes when we get to America.'

"But as it came to pass, when we finally did reach Montreal, Jackie was still in a bad condition. The inspector for

CONSULAT DE RUSSIE A BUCAREST

PASSEPORT

Il est porté à la connaissance de tous ceux à qui il appartient que le porteur du présent citoyen est *Ben*

Axelrod .... âgé de *39* ans

originaire de *Tetiev*

district *Taraschia* gouvernement *Kiew*

.... se rend *au Canada*

accompagné de sa femme *Liza* âgée de *36* ans

ses fils .... ses filles

Moris âgé de *15* ans *Rebeca* âgée de *17* ans

Zusif âgé de *8* ans *Leia* âgée de *9* ans

.... âgé de ..... ans .... âgée de ..... ans

.... âgé de ..... ans .... âgée de ..... ans

En foi de quoi lui a été délivré le présent passeport par le Consulat de Russie à Bucarest.

Valable pour un an,

Bucarest, Le *7/20 avril* 1923.

LE CONSUL

Consul de Russie certifie que la photographie et la signature ci-dessus sont celles du titulaire du présent passeport.

Bucarest, le *20 avril* 1923

LE CONSUL

At last: The family's passport to The Golden Land

ПАСПОРТЪ

Объявляется черезъ сіе всѣмъ и каждому, кому о томъ вѣдать надлежитъ, что предъявитель сего русскій гражданинъ *Беня*

Аксельродъ 39 лѣтъ,

уроженецъ *Тетіевъ*

уѣзда *Таращанскаго* *Кіевской*

~~губерніи~~ отправляется *въ Канаду*

въ сопровожденіи: своей жены *Лиза* 30 лѣтъ

сыновей			дочерей	
Морисъ	15 лѣтъ		*Ребека*	17 лѣтъ
Іосифъ	8 ~~мѣсяц~~ лѣтъ		*Лая*	9 лѣтъ
	лѣтъ			лѣтъ
	лѣтъ			лѣтъ

Во свидѣтельство сего данъ *ему*

сей паспортъ отъ Россійскаго Консульства въ Букарестѣ.

Дѣйствителенъ въ теченіе одного года

г. БУКАРЕСТЪ *7 Апрѣля* 1923 года.

Консулъ: *А. Барантовъ*

health comes on board the ship, takes one look at Jackie and says we can't get off. Every day this man comes and again examines Jackie. Four more days we have to wait before the inspector says Jackie is well enough."

"After everything, still you must wait?" Sylvia asks, perplexed.

"Three long years since Tetiev," says Ben, "we are running, hiding, working, making plans. Compared to that, a few days more is like wondering if you have a flea in the navel. And such is the way we come to this Golden Land."

"Say goodnight to Uncle Ben now, Sister," Morris says.

"Yes, Papa. Goodnight, Uncle Ben."

"Bear hug," he says, enfolding her in his strong arms. "Goodnight, little mama."

"Get to bed now before I give you a good potch on the tochis," Morris says, spanking her playfully.

Chapter 5

THE SOUP

HAS MANY EYES

"Try this good soup, Papa," says Berney, blowing on a spoonful of chicken broth and holding it out to Shimin. "Look how many eyes swim in the bowl," he says, pointing to the globules of fat. "It'll put some meat on your bones."

Shimin sits resolute, his mouth unopened, but Berney is patient. Not so many years ago, under the floorboards of Yossip's barn, he learned the virtue of waiting.

It is 1925. Berney, next-to-youngest of the brothers, is twenty-seven, Shimin sixty-four. Shimin, Berney and his wife Pauline live on the third floor of Morris's home in Chicago.

With great effort, Shimin tries to swallow. A trickle of soup dribbles from his mouth, and Berney dabs it off with a corner of the napkin that is tucked into Shimin's striped pajama shirt.

"Enough, enough," Shimin says hoarsely. "In Russia, I run a

foundry business. Many men work for me. I am a respected man. Now I can't even eat my own soup."

"Just until you get better, Papa."

"Better? The cancer gets better, the man gets worse," he says weakly. "At least in Russia our family is together. Now they're here, there—some half a country away; some across the ocean. Here I can't understand the language. I can't even talk to my own grandchildren. And this you call living?"

"Papa," Berney says, dipping another spoonful of soup and holding it up to Shimin's lips. "We have a home with Morris now. We're safe. No more pogroms. No more running."

Shimin raises his hand to signal he is finished and averts his head from the spoon. His head drops back onto the pillows that prop him up. Beneath the thin skin at his temple, a blue vein ticks slowly.

"Back in Russia, such a life my Chana and I have together, God rest her soul. Many sons, our precious daughter, Roochel," he says as he remembers the table, the vodka, his fervent prayers.

"So beautiful, my Chana. Like a rose. Her eyes—shining blue pieces of sky. And can she tell a story! A sailor would blush! She cooks, she raises our children, she makes life happy. Then her wagon upsets on the ice, and she is thrown out. Who would think such a thing could happen? But then, who would think that one day I make vats for the sugar mills and the next day hide in them? It shouldn't come to pass. But it does. I'm glad my Chana, God rest her soul, didn't live to see me like this."

"You lived through worse, Papa. You'll live through this."

"Let me tell you something, my son," Shimin says, raising

a bony finger. "When a man is fated to drown, he will drown even in a spoonful of water. Go take your soup and peddle it elsewhere. Now I will think of my Chana." He closes his eyes.

"All right, Papa. You rest. Later you'll eat." Berney slips out the extra pillow that elevates Shimin, brings the sheet up, smooths it under his chin and checks to make sure the window is tightly closed against drafts. He adjusts the heavy burgundy drapes and glances at Shimin to make sure that there is no glare. The stretched hollow parchment of his father's skin is almost as white as the linen pillowcase, but sleep erases the strain from his countenance. It is gentle, almost beatific. Berney tiptoes over, leans down and lightly kisses his father's forehead. Then he gathers up the tray and closes the door softly behind him.

Smooth the sheets, shut the window, adjust the drapes. Faint gestures in the face of so much want. Again and again, we learn how little control we have over the dice roll of the day—whether it's cancer or a cold, rampaging Cossacks or crabby kids. But as the dung beetle crawls down our collar, we do have choices: we can tremble, rage, shut down or make the soup. The snag is that how we act or react depends on how we see—all those little dots of light somersaulting into our brain, to be focused and filled in according to what we believe and whether we had a good night's sleep or not.

From an early age, perspective has been a struggle for me. When I was about seven, I looked into the bathroom mirror and saw my head shrink, telescoping down like Alice in Wonderland. It shriveled until it was no bigger than the head of a housefly, wing-preening on the windowsill, its bulging compound eyes breaking the world into small bits.

Mother took me to an eye doctor. In the darkened room, I peered at a bright screen as he clicked lens after lens in front of my eyes and quizzed: "Bigger or smaller? Clear or fuzzy? Better or worse?" When it was determined that I didn't need glasses, I kept my shrinking head to myself and, as much as possible, avoided mirrors. Hardly a loss, since mirrors reflect only what we choose to see.

Shimin sipped a little soup that evening and went to sleep. The next morning, Sylvia, ready to leave for school in her white blouse with puffed sleeves and her navy jumper, comes in to kiss her father Morris good-bye.

"Papa?"

"Yes, Sister?" Morris says, looking up from the green lines of the account ledger for his lumber company, where he costs out supplies and does sums in his head as quickly as a calculator.

"Papa, last night Grandpa couldn't swallow his bread pudding."

"Your grandpa, he's a very sick man," Morris says, patting Sylvia's cheek. "But you must always remember, Sister, even the worst life is better than the best death. And whether you are sick or starving, whether you are spit on or beaten, right down to the brink of the grave you must still hope and be brave. Now be a good girl and learn a lot at school," he says, kissing her.

Just as the bustle of the many members of the household settles into routine, Berney's wife, Pauline, a woman of dainty demeanor and Rubenesque proportions, her dark bobbed hair in disarray, comes downstairs calling in a quaking voice, "Morris, Morris. Quickly! Come quickly!"

Morris turns white and jumps up from the table. Compressed by a sturdy, compact physique, his energy explodes from him more times than not.

"What happened?"

"Papa, it's Papa. He doesn't speak."

"What do you mean, he doesn't speak?" He rushes up the stairs behind Pauline. "In his throat he has cancer, how much would you be talking?"

"It's not like that," she says excitedly. She fumbles for the handkerchief tucked into the belt of her dress.

"An old man and his dreams," Morris mutters under his breath as they race up the second flight. He flings open the door to his father's room.

"Papa," he says, walking quickly to the bed and sitting down on the edge. He picks up Shimin's shrunken, waxy hand and pats it. "Papa, wake up, wake up."

With no response, he pats Shimin's cheek briskly. "Wake up, Papa, wake up." Then he leans down and puts his head on Shimin's chest and listens. Slowly he sits up. Tears well in his blue eyes and spill over onto his cheeks. "He ends his days," he whispers.

"Blessed be the True Judge," Pauline says, weeping.

After several minutes of sobbing, Morris takes a handkerchief from his pocket and blows his nose.

"What happened, tell me what happened?" he asks hoarsely.

"I go to take Papa a little oatmeal, some prune juice, some tea," she says, still breathless. "I set down the tray by his bed and wake him. Slowly, he gets up and stumbles over to the mirror.

Berney and his wife, Pauline

He strokes his beard and squints. Such a long time he looks. Then he rasps, '*Ich bin shoein nisht kein mensch,* I am no longer a person.' He turns around and walks back to his bed like a man with too much wine. He lays down, his eyes close, he takes a deep breath, his eyebrows lift as if he's reaching high in his head for a dream. Then he gasps, and like a wrinkled shirt, he goes limp." Pauline bites her lip and tries to gulp back her sobs.

Morris gets up. "I'll go make arrangements," he says, squeezing Pauline's shoulder.

"No longer a person," Shimin said. At what point is that? When pain becomes unbearable? When the unknown seems better than the known? When we no longer have questions? When we lose our mind? Body? Spirit?

Webster defines *person* as "a human being as distinguished from an animal or thing." Oddly enough, the word itself is derived from the Latin *persona,* or "mask."

Josh, you probably don't remember a neighborhood party we went to close to Halloween time when you were about three. One of the older kids, Todd, came through the living room wearing a mask. Was it a pirate or some celebrity of the day? You looked at the plastic face with intense curiosity and inquired, "Who is that?"

"A masked man," I said.

Masked Man came through the visiting group several times, fascinating you each time, then disappeared.

After a while, you asked, "What happened to mask man?"

"He broke," Todd replied.

"Where did he go?"

"I threw him in the garbage," Todd said.

We bobbed for apples, drank cider, ate popcorn and then went home. As I was trying to tuck you in (way past your bedtime), our conversation was like a broken record.

"What happened to mask man?"

"The mask broke."

"Where did mask man go?"

"Todd threw it out."

"Why did he throw mask man away?"

"Because the mask was broken."

"Couldn't Todd fix mask man?"

"I guess not. Josh, it's time to go to bed now."

"Mommy?"

"Last question, Josh."

"If I broke, would you throw me in the garbage?"

An arrow to the heart—one of those moments when a parent's shrouded eyes jerk wide with a vision of long ago—that forgotten place where everything shines, where everything quakes. Masks have people behind them. You understood that. But what I didn't understand was that for you, the mask was as real as the person, no less imbued with power and life than a Tibetan spirit mask.

When each of you was born, Josh and Jonny, I was dumbfounded by the panoply of expressions that flickered over your sleeping countenances from day one. Terror, sadness, surprise, pain, bliss. Not modeled behavior but something inherent, the same way that your brand-new feet—fresh from nine months of treading water—still smelled distinctly like feet.

And when flesh falls away? What then? Does something essential linger? Something unique as the sworls at the tips of our fingers? Or is it all back to biblical darkness; to the uncreated?

Are we poster children of the Zen saying, "One drop of water holds the taste of the seven seas"?

When we are born, we scrutinize for connection—his father's eyes, her mother's chin, the Axelrood build. But by the time we die, we cleave to selfhood. The collective community mourns not the multitude we embodied, but idiosyncrasy, accomplishment, a particular constellation of moles on our skin. Our society commemorates its dead with chiseled headstones; a final fill-in-the-blanks form with name, birth day, family role—husband, wife, child—and that previously unknown date. But under a dusky emerald canopy elsewhere, an indigenous rain forest people sanctify their loved ones in a more visceral ritual. And perhaps more true to nature. After they burn the body, pulverize the bones and mix the grind with liquid, they drink it. Ultimate communion. We hold the departed in our hearts, not just because we remember them, but because we *are* them.

"Such a funeral," says Pauline, taking off her coat and hanging it in the entry closet. "Even Papa Shimin, God rest his soul, would have enjoyed the rabbi." She chokes up as new tears appear on her already streaked face. "Here, Lisa, let me take your coat for you. You sit. You've been too long on that ankle of yours."

"Thank you, Pauline," says Lisa. "Jackie, Dick! Stop with the running! Where do you think you go so fast? Haste is good only for catching fleas. Slow down! Show some respect! Come here, boys, give me your coats." She unbuttons little Jackie's coat, stroking his cheek that still bears the fading burn scars. Going to the closet, she hangs up his coat while ten-year-old

Sylvia helps her little brother Dick take off his. Then Lisa hobbles over to the davenport and sits down with a sigh on the plump cushions.

"Bill!" Uncle Berney scolds Sylvia's older brother. "What are you doing?" Berney drapes the cloth back over the hall mirror. Following tradition, all the mirrors in the house have been covered. "Do you want that the Angel of Death should see you?"

"I was just looking to see where my suit jacket is torn," Bill says, probing the hole with his finger and contorting as he tries to see his shoulder.

"There's nothing to see but a rip, boychik. It's not something you see, it's something you feel. We make a hole in our clothes to be the sign of what's in here." Berney thumps his chest as tears roll down his cheeks. "Come now, eat. Everybody brings food. Boiled eggs, potatoes, peas, lentils. Come."

"But I don't like boiled eggs or lentils. Why do we have to eat eggs?"

"He doesn't like eggs. What are we going to do with you, boychik? Don't you know anything? Round food. We eat round food to mourn those who have passed on. From dust we come, to dust we go. The circle of eternal life."

"Aunt Lisa, Aunt Lisa!" Sylvia says, running over to Lisa.

"What is it, Sister?" Lisa says, dabbing her eyes and blowing her nose.

"I need to talk to you," Sylvia whispers urgently.

"So talk, bubbelah."

"Not here."

"All right. We go into the kitchen." As Lisa gets up, she straightens the lace antimacassar on the armrest of the davenport and fluffs the cushion.

The kitchen counters are crowded with breads, casseroles covered with snowy linen tea towels—lentils, kasha, noodle kugels; plates of cookies—almond, macaroons, mandelbrot.

"So what's the matter, Sister?"

"Aunt Lisa, Dickie didn't put his on," Sylvia says, trembling.

"Didn't put his what on, bubbelah? What could be so terrible?"

"Now he's going to follow us home!" She begins to cry.

"Who's going to follow?"

"Papa said Grandpa would follow us home from the cemetery if we didn't put a pebble on his gravestone. And Dickie put his in his pocket. I just saw him playing with it," she says, sobbing.

"His pebble? Oy! Faygeleh, faygeleh, my little bird, is that what you cry about?"

Lisa sits on a kitchen chair and takes Sylvia on her lap.

"One little stone from one little boy will not matter. Grandpa, may he rest in peace, will stay right where he is. Whenever you need him, all you have to do is ask. You have a question, you have a problem, you need advice, Grandpa will be there. Just like you helped take care of him these last years, now he will look after you. Like the rabbi says in the Kaddish, *Yis-gad-dal v'yis-kad-dash sh'meh rab-bo*—May their memory be a blessing to those who cherish it.

"Achh, here in Die Goldeneh Medina, what do you children know about death? Believe me, faygeleh, one little pebble will not matter. Dry now the eyes," Lisa says, fishing in her pocket for a clean hanky. "Such pretty blue eyes," she says, dabbing them. "Plenty of time for tears when we sit shivah for Grandpa. Seven days we pray and weep. Now let's get a little something to eat and drink. Even to make tears, you need to eat. This I know. Come, bubbelah. Everything's all right with you now?"

"Yes, Aunt Lisa. I'm all right now. I was just scared."

Lisa inhales deeply and exhales a portion of the air in the manner of all who wait—part of every breath held back in constant vigilance.

"Scared, faygeleh?" She pats Sylvia's back, her eyes fixed in the distance. "Of course you're scared. What else should you be? Everybody gets scared. Scared is part of living."

It's true, Josh and Jonny, at least for me, when Lisa says, "Here in Die Goldeneh Medina, what do you children know about death?" Here I am, fifty, and the only death I've experienced firsthand is that of Chita, our dog. Grandpa Morris; my father; Dad's mother and father; all died at a distance. They were packaged deaths, like store-bought food neatly sealed off from smell, feel, the potency of ripeness, the weight of fallen flesh.

When Chita died, Dad was in Iowa burying his father. Josh, you were away at college; and you, Jonny, who used to climb out of your crib and curl up underneath it to sleep alongside Chita, were unable to face the death of your heart-mate, security blanket, protector and confidante of fifteen years. You said your good-byes earlier that evening, then left with your buddies.

It was pitch-black, cold and raining. By flashlight, the only way of judging the depth of the hole as I dug was to step in and see how far down it took me. I could not believe how deep it was, deeper than I had ever known possible. I stood behind our shed in that black pit and stabbed out shovelsful from the hard November ground.

All the comfort phrases, reasoned philosophies and grappling hooks of faith were elsewhere in well-lit places, not here. My coat got soiled carrying Chita and laying her in place. I set her in one way, with her head toward the field where she loved to run, and then changed her the other way. Honestly, I don't remember which way I finally settled on. All I know is that at the time, it really mattered. I scooped up the first shovel of dirt to cover her up and couldn't. I was afraid I'd plug up her nostrils and she wouldn't be able to breathe. I had to go inside and get something to blanket her first.

Now I understand why the ancients buried food, clothing and furniture with their dead, why suttees leaped into the pyres of their burning husbands, why we lay something precious over the heart or into the hand of those we bury. It's our last chance to throw graspable love into the void, to spit in the eye of the unknown.

I can't begin to imagine scraping the earth with my bare hands, as Lisa did, and placing one of you in it. That would be more incomprehensible than life itself.

Life. This thin-skinned sack we carry from place to place that gurgles and pukes; that rages and laughs and leaks; this incomprehensible "infinite in a grain of sand" that can be snuffed in a blink.

It is too much to be given. It is too much to bear. It is too much to lose.

And yet we do, with every breath.

Chapter 6

THE PASSOVER

WHAT'S ALL THIS pssst-psssst-psssst that goes on between you children?" asks Morris.

It's early spring in Chicago, 1929. They are at the door of Ben and Lisa's apartment behind the Cedar Hand Laundry.

"Nothing, Papa," says Sylvia, stifling the adolescent giggle of a fourteen-year-old and casting an impish look at her brothers Bill and Dick.

"With such whispering a 'nothing' becomes a 'something,'" Morris says, waiting for an answer with raised brows and a steady gaze. "Sister?"

"It's not very polite, Papa."

"So? Out with it, already."

"We were just saying that Aunt Lisa makes the best Passover dinner of anyone."

Morris smiles, his eyes crinkling at the corners.

"Mmm, it smells good even out here," Dick says, jiggling excitedly at the door.

Suddenly, Morris scowls at Bill, leans over, grabs both of his shoulders and begins to shake him. "And you. You behave yourself this year. No more noshing off everybody's plates before the seder. May your hands dry up if you ever again gonif charoses from your brother and sister. You won't have a hand left to feed yourself. Understand?"

"Yes, Papa," Bill says penitently, head lowered.

"Good. It's settled." Morris lets go and smooths down the shoulders of Bill's suit as the door opens.

"Morris, Sister, boys," says Uncle Ben. "Gut Yontif!"

There is a din of holiday greetings along with hugs and kisses.

"Come in, come in."

In the living room, more aunts, uncles and cousins. More Gut Yontifs.

In the bedroom, little Dick whispers as they take off their coats. "Sister, what's charoses?"

"Don't you remember? The chopped-up apples and nuts and cinnamon and sugar all mixed together with a little wine. Remember?"

"Oh, yes. Charoses, yum!"

"And do you remember what the charoses symbolizes?"

"No."

"Think, Dick, think. Why do we celebrate Passover?"

"Because God let the Angel of Death pass over the house of the Jews."

"Yes. What else?" Sylvia, ever the teacher, presses.

"Because God sent *plagues*! Frogs! And blood! And *bugs*!"

"Yes. And . . . ? What kind of bread?"

"Matzoh!"

"Yes. We eat matzoh, unleavened bread, because the bread didn't have time to rise before we escaped. When we were slaves of Pharaoh, God let Moses part the Red Sea and deliver us from the land of Egypt and then let the Red Sea swallow up all the soldiers who chased after us. So we eat charoses to remember what?"

"Tears?"

"No, not tears. That's the salt water we dip the egg in. Salt water for tears. Tears of the oppressed. Egg for the promise of new life."

"I don't like horseradish, Sister. Do I have to eat the horseradish?"

"You don't have to eat all of it," Sylvia says, straightening her younger brother's tie, "but you have to take a taste to remember the bitter days when we were slaves and had to build for Pharaoh. And what do you use when you build? What makes the bricks stick together, Dick?"

"Mortar! Charoses!"

"That's right," she says, licking her fingertips and slicking down his hair. "See. You can figure it out if you just think a minute."

Morris comes in. "What are you hooligans still doing in here?" he says. "Everybody asks where you are. Come on."

"I don't want to," Dick says, cringing.

"Why not?"

"Aunt Sophie pinches my cheek too hard!"

"That's because she loves you," Morris says with a chuckle. "Come on now. Be a mensch!" He braces Dick with little slaps on the cheek.

"I'm going to the kitchen to see if Aunt Lisa needs help," says Sylvia, quickly detouring.

"On your way, make sure your brother Bill doesn't make mischief in the dining room," Morris warns, little Dick in reluctant tow.

"Yes, Papa."

"Gut Yontif, Aunt Lisa, Gut Yontif, Aunt Pauline," says Sylvia, entering the kitchen. "Gut Yontif, Cousin Rae."

The steamy air is heavy with the smell of fat-laden chicken broth, garlic, onions, freshly starched clothing, eau de cologne, horseradish, sweet stewed prunes. The women bee-dance around pots and platters. In the buzz and heat of this inner sanctum, Sylvia feels woozy, excited, at home.

"Sister! Gut Yontif," Aunt Lisa says, wiping her hands on a towel and pressing Sylvia hard to her bosom. Releasing her, Lisa's eyes shine as she scrutinizes Sylvia's chest. "Such a beautiful young woman you get to be, a shayne maidel. Pauline, look! Our Sister—a shayne maidel."

Sylvia feels embarrassment flood her face. "May I help with anything, Aunt Lisa?" (Her grammar is impeccable, as you well know, Josh and Jonny, even as a young girl.)

"Help? Of course! Here. Put on this apron so you don't mess the pretty dress. Then with the spoon you can mix up the beet salad. Roasted chicken's almost ready," Lisa says as she squints in the blast of heat from the oven and bastes it one last time.

"Rae," she instructs her oldest daughter, now twenty-two, "you go pour wine. Make sure everyone has a Haggadah, a prayer book—except for the children. They share. Here, take the matzoh to the living room. Make sure all the children eat a little nosh. It's so long with the prayers, with the songs, with the whole Passover story. By the time we get to dinner, they chomp at the bit. And little Seymour's pants. Make sure you check before the seder to see if Seymour makes a pish in his pants."

"Yes, Mameh."

"Sister, did you get a little nosh of something?"

"Not yet, Aunt Lisa."

"Here. Take some of this chopped egg on a little matzoh."

"Mmmm. Thank you, Aunt Lisa."

"Pauline. The fish? How does the fish come?"

"Boiled just nice. Ready for the horseradish," says Pauline, concentrating as she lifts the carp from the pot and gently positions it on a warm platter. She smiles as she tucks sprigs of parsley around it.

"Oy," Lisa says. "I forget to turn down the carrot tsimmes. Oh, Sophie. Good. You're here." Sophie and Mike and their three children have come from New York for Passover.

"What can I do?"

"Sophie, stir the carrots and prunes so they shouldn't burn. Turn way down with the fire—the smallest flame. Ohh. And taste. Tell me what it still needs." Sophie stirs, carefully extracts a carrot slice on the tip of the spoon, blows, puts it in her mouth and chews thoughtfully.

"A little more cinnamon," she says, smacking her lips repeatedly. "Just a touch." She takes a bit from the jar and sprinkles its fragrance into the pot. "So, Lisa? What did the new doctor say about your ankle?"

"What should he say? Like every doctor, he gives me some new schmear to put on the sore." She looks down at her bandaged leg. "If I had money for every doctor I see, I'd be a rich woman."

"Achh. I look like I'm shvitzing in a steam bath with all this heat," Pauline says, wiping her forehead with the corner of her apron.

"So?" says Lisa. "Why should this night be different from all other nights?" They all chuckle at Lisa's joke, an echo of the Passover questions that the youngest child at the seder has to memorize and recite. "*Mah-nish ta-nah-ha-lai-law hazeh mee-kawl ha-lay-los?* Why is this night different from all other nights?"

Lisa goes on, "Seven A.M. to nine o'clock at night, we sweat doing laundry. Wash, iron, make with the bundles, deliver. But so far (knock on wood, no evil eye), it goes. We eat. We pay the bills. We buy for the children. Every week, a little we put away so they go to a good college."

"Aunt Lisa?"

"Here, Sister. Stir this borscht while you make with the questions."

"Aunt Lisa, is it true that Jackie got to drive the wagon when Uncle Ben was a peddler?"

Lisa laughs. "Jackie told you that?"

"Yes. Was he really old enough to drive?"

"Sometimes Jackie did go with his papa," Lisa says as she scoops beet salad from a wooden mixing bowl into a cut crystal dish. "Together they clip and clop up and down the alleys.

Ben calls, 'Apples, potatoes!' Little Jackie makes echo, 'Appuls, tatoes!' And, yes, sometimes Ben lets Jackie hold the reins of the horse. But drive the wagon all by himself? No. Achh—my poor Ben. Fourteen hours a day he peddles. He's not so young anymore. Forty-two—not a spring chicken. But thank God, we get enough money from peddling, and from your papa, Sister—from Morris, a blessing on his head—to open this hand-laundry business. Now Jackie can make like the big man delivering shirts."

"Here, Sister," Pauline says, coming over. "When you stir, don't make round and round. Go like this. See? Like the number 8. You draw with your spoon the number 8 in the pot. That keeps from burning the soup, the custard, whatever you cook."

"Like this, Aunt Pauline?"

"That's right."

"Why is a figure 8 better than round and round?"

"Listen to her," Pauline says, chucking Sylvia proudly under the chin. "Such a smart girl. For every answer, a new question. It's better because you get more from your stir that way."

"See?" says Sophie. "You learn something new, Sister. Every day, something new to learn." She fishes up the stray hairs clinging to her neck and pins them back. "So what else needs doing?"

"Let me think . . . ," Lisa says. "Borscht, beet salad, fish, chicken, applesauce, tsimmes, walnut cake. No. It's all done. We're ready to make seder," Lisa says, removing her apron and smoothing her dress. "Sister, you go announce that everyone should come to the table."

"The whole mishpocheh," Ben says, beaming as everyone crowds around the table. Two places, set with plates and wine cups, remain empty.

"Who sits there?" Dick whispers to Sylvia.

"You always set a place for Elijah the Prophet," Sylvia tells him. "Every Passover. We pour wine into his cup and invite him in. That's who we open the door for during the seder, hoping he will come."

"And the other place?"

"That's for Anna," Sylvia whispers. "Aunt Lisa sets a place so Anna will come, too."

Lisa lights the candles. They hiss briefly and flicker as their flame grows taller and brighter. She gathers their light into her heart and softly blesses the household, all those present and all whom the heart remembers. Everyone is illumined by a special radiance. On the faces of the adults, the deep lines of worry and struggle, suffering and endless work, seem suffused into something holy. The children shine with promise. And everyone is there. Faraway relatives in Russia, New York, Canada. Relatives now gone—Chana, Shimin, Roochel, Ben and Lisa's baby, and little Anna. In these cramped living quarters in back of the Cedar Hand Laundry, for a brief flickering moment, all are reunited. All are at peace.

More for your stir from a figure 8 . . . could the same be said of family? Connected circles offer more than solitary ones?

The recipe for the human condition hasn't changed much from the beginning—wake, eat, procreate, sleep, pay the piper, make way for the next generation. Add in some torments and tickles. Mix together with pain, bliss, terrible choices, love, compromise. Char over a primitive fire or serve from the microwave, but at the bone, it's no different.

When you were born, Jonny, I secretly worried that I wouldn't have enough love for you. I loved Dad and Josh so much it hurt. How could I love you as much too? After nine months, this intimate stranger, this womb mystery who sprouted limbs and hair and man parts, came forth, smush-faced, squinting against the light. The nurse held you just beyond my reach.

"Check to see that all his fingers and toes are there," she instructed me crisply, rotating you for inspection like a roast at the meat counter. Was this meant to be some kind of assurance in a world where everything must add up? A world where numbers count and cause has effect? Fiercely impatient, I grabbed. It was weight that mattered. Warm ballast that anchored me to the quiet center.

Josh and Jonny, you have taken me to places of rapture and discovery I never dreamed I could go. My fear-filled heart learned to bear pain and joy so excruciating it imploded into a new organ, elasticized with courage.

But for me, by far the most brutal part of family is not the sleepless nights, the worry, the miscommunications, misdeeds, misguided decisions. It's that you brought me face-to-face with my own defects. No matter how often I avert my eyes from mirrors, when I look at you two, I see vestiges of my reflection. A tilt of the head, a gesture, the triggers and tender spots exposed. I recognize the flaws I try to overlook in myself.

No wonder the solitary life of a hermit has always tempted

me. Fall short of purpose, and hurt only yourself. I strive to center but am drawn away by taste, smell, sound, sight, touch; summer evenings tinctured with honeysuckle, Bach, the tiny heaven of forget-me-nots with their perfect blue centered with a sun. I envision stitching my eyelids shut, plugging my ears and nostrils, sealing my lips. But like a naughty child at hide-and-seek, I know I would peek, because at the core I'm like you, Josh, when you were little. You used to bolt from your bath, jump naked onto the fuzzy comforter on our bed and roll around. I once called you a little sybarite. From then on, you would exclaim as you undulated, "Sysaripe, sysaripe."

Sybarite of the senses, I'm dazzled like you, Jonny, the night you stood outside slowly circling. "Look, look," you rhapsodized. "Stars everywhere! Stars in the trees! Stars in the sky! Stars in the grass!" Stars hung unthinkably low. Fireflies had risen inconceivably high. They mingled so you could not riddle ancient light from present.

As a child, I too remember stars that seemed so close, I knew I could reach out and pluck one if only my toes could lift me a little higher, my arms rubberband a little longer. Lured by the glimmer just beyond reach, I ran inside to get a broom, to give me added length. As I was sweeping the sky on tiptoe, to my amazement a silvery shower rained over my head. Scrambling to catch the shimmer, I realized that my brother George had shadowed behind me and shaken a box of gummed silver-paper stars over my head.

But it is neither real nor paper-star radiance that hampers my focus. It is my own distractibility. Even when I retreat from the hubbub of family to the solitude of the woods, it is not hush that holds me but jittering white gnats, shag-barked evergreens, prismatic spider webs, wild strawberry leaves indiscernible when rubbed between my fingers because their leaves so resemble skin, the cry of a wood thrush ringing my body like crystal on the brink of shatter. Tangled roots writhe above the forest floor. To chop at a root because it protrudes, to extricate one artery, which tree might be wounded?

Our own circle connects to family, known or unknown, biological or chosen, a Möbius strip twisted into continuum—the struggles, the vista, the undertow, the love.

"More for your stir." Lay the figure 8 on its side, and you have the symbol for infinity.

Chapter 7

ANNA

NOT TOO FAR FROM TETIEV, in the one-room house of the woman who procured her from the watchman's wife in trade for a woolen shawl, is little Anna. It is 1919.

As Anna tilts her head to one side and then the other, shapes appear in the swirly, smoke-smudged whitewash of the ceiling. A bird. A pickle. A horse. A woman with a babushka on her head.

Do you ever do that, Jonny and Josh? The edges of my childhood shimmied with mirage. Pictures lurked in the carpet nubble; phantasmagoria in the clouds.

One of my earliest recollections echoes Anna's. We lived in Houston, Texas, in an apartment on Bonnie Brae Street. My room was paneled in a yellowy varnished knotty pine that was punctuated with growth rings and blotches. Every night I would stare at these hypnotically. One knot, ringed with wavy concentric circles, whirlpooled into a gnarled old witch lady with an elongated head. There was a cat too, its bushy tail upright and tapered like a conifer. And a pointy-capped clown with a dubious grin—leer, really. I remember searching with some desperation for friendlier folk. The witch lady and the clown scared me, though I had some sense, even at three, that the appearance and disappearance of these phantoms were somewhat in my own control.

Yet even now I can be idly gazing at a rug, or looking blankly at the wall of a roadstop restroom, and there it is— an image develops before my eyes like a Polaroid picture. Sometimes I wonder about this need to turn mirage and evanescence into something as solid and graspable as a doorknob or a frying pan. Perhaps they are merely Rorschachs of a pretelevision childhood. Do you see them, too? It excites and dismays me to think that members of the same family keep so many untold and hidden stories from each other.

But the day that Anna saw shapes in the ceiling swirls, she was neither approaching sleep, nor in a familiar room.

Under the wooden bench, two other children are squashed beside her, whispering, but she can't understand them. A bullet from a skirmish outside whizzes through the one window of the izba and strikes the timber wall. Shards of glass scatter everywhere. "I don't like it here," Anna says. "I'm leaving."

Then she cries, "Owww!"

She blinks and reaches back to the back of her head where it hurts. She doesn't remember being thrown against the wall as she tried to leave. Nor much of anything else.

"Aiyee!" she whimpers as wet leaves are pressed against the back of her head. She catches a warning look from the stern woman who holds the dripping wad.

"Manya," another woman says. "Poultice her head morning and night. It draws out the bad blood."

What are they saying? Anna wonders. She only understands Yiddish. The one with the blue eyes and blond hair, the one called Manya, moves quickly as she takes a sourish mash of leaves steeping in a bowl of hot water and squeezes it in her meaty fist. She takes off the old leaves from Anna's head and applies new ones. They sear like a hot poker. Anna starts to cry, but feels her shoulder clamped with a powerful grip. She snuffles down her tears and swallows hard. At last, the ministerings are over, and she is free to get up and join the other two children. The shooting over, they run outside from the one-room house.

The day is so bright, it makes Anna's eyes ache. New grass shimmers like green fire. Her bare feet sting with cold, but the sun-warmed breeze caresses her legs and arms and fills her with bounce despite her throbbing head. Once she had shoes. Where are they? No matter. The other children don't have any either.

The air is rich with the smell of thawing manure, unleashed green and the peppery dust of chickens, pigs and horses that hold long months of winter in their fur and feathers. Anna sneezes. She watches a swaybacked chestnut pony tug up tufts of grass and crunch resonantly, khaki drool oozing over its freckled, fleshy lips. The other children run ahead, shouting.

"Olga, Olga!" the boy calls. The small girl with sandy hair, only a few years older than Anna, runs over to him. "Vasil," she says. The boy is a bit taller and looks older than Olga, a pale stick figure with unruly brown hair and kind, knowing eyes. Both speak Russian. They confer momentarily, then motion little Anna to come.

Pointing to several chickens that nest on a pile of straw,

Vasil slowly approaches, reaches underneath a chicken and brings out a large brown egg. He hands it to Anna. She cradles the smooth, satisfying shape and feels its delicious heat spread through her limbs to a place deep inside. She looks at Olga and Vasil, beaming. They all laugh, a language she can understand, and after collecting a few more eggs, they leave the broody hens to their hatching.

When they return to the house, Anna hungrily eyes a round of rye bread on the table where they deposit the eggs and reaches for a crumb fallen from the gritty loaf. But the children signal a warning against it. It doesn't take long for her to learn that the scant food in the household is portioned and served only by Manya. Even when Manya is gone from dawn until evening, they are forbidden to touch a morsel.

Olga and Vasil lead Anna to a lopsided lean-to outside the house, where they gather up tools and head out along a rutted field. They move together, three children aged two, five and seven, stumbling over the rocks and dirt toward Manya, who is jabbing with her hoe at cold earthen clods. Each child takes a place along the row with Anna at the end. Manya does the heavy breaking, then moves up. Vasil follows behind her, further pulverizing the dirt. Then come Olga and Anna, who smooth out and mound the dirt. Their earlier joy vanishes as they work doggedly alongside Manya.

After a while, Vasil stops to examine the palm of his hand, some cut or splinter perhaps, Anna cannot tell. Manya scolds him and soundly cuffs his cheeks, first one, then the other. When Olga's energy flags, she is scolded, too. But strangely, Anna escapes these outbursts, both now and, for the most part, in the years that follow.

The sun, and any residue of warmth, fades behind a stand of larch trees before Manya leads the tired children home. The children return the tools to the shed and, shivering, take their turn in the outhouse.

Before entering the house with its one room serving as kitchen, bedroom, living room and dining room, Olga and Vasil stand like ghostly crickets, rubbing first one foot, then the other, up and down the opposite leg to remove crumbles of dirt. Anna follows suit.

While the potatoes boil on the stove, Manya sets out five plates, three with a small chunk of bread and an egg-sized lump of fermented cabbage, two with larger portions. Vasil pours water into metal cups, one for the children to share, one for Manya and one for Sergei, Manya's husband. When the potatoes are done, they are dished onto the plates, steaming in watery puddles. Anna struggles between letting the warm vapor bathe her numb face or gulping down the hot mass. Her stomach wins.

Mealtime is a quick and silent affair. As she sits there with an empty plate, she has a faded memory of before the scary time, before Papa left her with all those people. She remembers sitting at a table with talking and laughing, and the passing of bowls, and hands patting her and scooping a little of this and a little of that onto her plate, urging her to eat.

Her reverie is short-lived as they each get up and carry their dishes over to a pail. Olga and Vasil wash the dishes as she watches, and finally, in an exhausted blur, Anna takes her place next to them on a worn red rug spread each night on the bare floor. Sergei and Manya make beds on the sitting benches in the summer and, during the colder months, as is the custom, atop the flat cookstove, which retains a lingering vestige of warmth.

Is it the heavy, rough wool blanket that weighs Anna down in dreamless sleep, or utter fatigue? Of nights she remembers little except those occasions, all too frequent, when Manya takes to vodka. Then no amount of weight, blankets or fatigue can muffle the screams and ragings as she and Sergei fight.

But most nights, she plunges so deeply into sleep that when she hears noise (as if from far away) and feels jostling, it takes every ounce of energy to gain buoyancy and surface into the weak light of morning.

For me it took years to discover what Anna learned early. That stamina, endurance and the knack of pulling myself from the suck of inertia get me through the day, not all those years spent in dorm rooms and library carrels studying earth science, postmodern literature and French grammar. I should have spent more time in gym shorts perfecting the hurdle, the broad jump, the sprint, the long shot, the marathon. Continued my ballet to give me practice for the balance in life, where truth and its opposite coexist. The point where the pressure of paradox is so intense, it leaves a trail of blood.

We read to learn; we learn so that we may know; we know in order to do. Anna skipped right to the "do."

"Come!" Manya orders the children one day in early summer when Anna is four. "Your grandmother has died." Manya's demeanor reflects not stoicism but the intense dislike she and her mother-in-law felt toward each other.

Olga, Vasil and Anna take turns under the bruising cloth

that Manya scours over their faces, arms and hands. She pulls the comb without mercy through hair tangles and plasters Vasil's cowlick down with water.

Then, wordless, they march down the hill path, adjacent to their property, to where the grandmother lived. Grandmother Lochotsky was not a frequent visitor to Manya's house nor they to hers, so to the silence there was added an air of strain.

"Oh," Anna wishes, "if only we could stop by the lake and catch fish or pull wild onion grass. Fish," she thinks, her mouth watering, "smoked and juicy from an outdoor fire." She sees its flesh flapped open, growing a translucent garden of tiny bones all in a row. But they don't stop. The procession continues past the lake to the squat, thatched-roof izba.

The wooden door opens on creaking hinges. Several people mill around inside, including Sergei, Manya's husband. It takes a few moments for Anna's eyes to adjust to the candle-lit gloom before she sees the body of the grandmother lying in a rude pine box on a bench in the middle of the room. Grandmother Lochotsky is dressed in black, her big-knuckled hands folded across her heart. The room smells of waxy smoke, cabbage and decay. All around there is a dense feeling of obstacle—like being in total darkness and sensing that there is a wall or tree in front of you.

"Children, kiss your grandmother's hands," Manya commands as she shoves Vasil close to the body. Stiffly, he bends and pecks his lips to the rough, prominent knuckles. As he straightens, his blue eyes are wide with revulsion.

"Now you," Manya says, pushing Olga forward.

"I'm afraid," Olga whimpers.

"Kiss her," Manya says, hefting Olga onto a little stool so she can reach.

"I don't want to," she cries.

"Show your respect," Manya says, cuffing her on the back. Paralyzed with fear, Olga continues to cry until Manya forces her head down to the old woman's folded hands. "Anna. Come."

Anna can barely hear Manya through the pounding whoosh of her heart. She feels Manya lift her up and tilt her, head down, in a nosedive into the corpse. Anna feels herself being swallowed, engulfed in a cold, damp, crawly place. She can't breathe, or hear or see. And it is with stunned surprise that she feels the feet of her stiffened legs jolt against the floor and the world come swimming back.

"Go now," Manya says. "Pull some radish and peel some potato for supper. Twelve radish. Seven potato."

The children, still shackled with dread, walk rigidly from the house.

Outside, in silent consensus, they bolt toward the lake, downhill all the way. Olga and Anna collapse close together on their stomachs amid the insect hum of the tall grass and listen to plunking pebbles that Vasil jettisons from the bank into the light-corrugated water. The earth is yielding and fragrant against Anna's cheek. She combs the sheened grasses between her fingers, and with each stroke, her small hands clutch the roots, feeling comfort in their hairlike resistance.

"Hurry! Before Mama comes," Vasil urges them. Olga gets up and brushes herself off, but Anna sleeps. "Anna, Anna, wake up."

In the years she's been with Manya, her chubby arms and legs have dwindled to reed. But here, on this warm bosom of earth, her whole body feels luscious, soft. Earth holds for Anna all that trauma and deprivation have erased.

"Wake up, Anna." Her long dark lashes flutter open to see Vasil and Olga hovering over her.

The children sprint uphill, stopping in the garden to pull radishes. The prickly-haired leaves make Anna's hands itch. She can hardly wait for tart, fleshy plums or sweet, crisp pears, but they are not ripe.

That night, even though there is no hint of chill to the air, the children press unusually close together, leaving no space for nightmares to enter their sleep. But they do. From that day and for years to come, the children, particularly Anna, have a frigid, goose-fleshed terror of Grandmother Lochotsky's house, especially as it becomes overgrown with weeds.

According to those in the know, the world of dreams and nightmares is a mishmosh of our daily doings and the brutish bilge below: part news commentator, part primal brain with its well-honed instinct for predator/prey and its claws and canines bared.

Still, at times we emerge from sleep with messages, presences, dirt under our fingernails from places we couldn't possibly know or fathom.

One night I wakened to distressed whimpers. On the floor, Chita was in dream, feet scrabbling frantically against the bedframe. No sooner had I groped down to quiet her heaving side, than you, Jonny, raced in from your room and hurled yourself into my arms. You were three. "Mommy, I had a night dream. A big bear grabbed Chita in its teeth and threw her in the creek. Then the bear comed to get me."

Coincidence? No more than waking to find that a loved one has died; a loved one who came in dream the night before to say good-bye.

Two more years pass for Anna, each season marked by its familiar tasks. She is six and speaks fluent Russian now. Because of her lovely looks, in milder seasons she is regularly forced to beg for coins outside the town church. But now it's winter and the children sit inside picking down from feathers to sell in the market.

With no winter clothes, no boots or coat, nothing more than the once-a-year shapeless shift for Olga and Anna and the rough-sack shirt and pants for Vasil, winter is an endless, drab rigor. A terrible draft knifes in under the door and from around the rags that stuff the broken windowpane. When urgency can no longer be endured, the children dash barefoot through the snow to the outhouse. The frigid wind vibrates their taut muscles and nerves, making their bones hum.

This day, Manya's been at the vodka. As she drinks, the harshness of life begins to haze. Vasil stations himself by the door to alert her of Sergei's arrival. Only one thing enrages Sergei more than finding her drunk: finding her with another man.

"Quickly! He comes," Vasil warns. But it's too late, and Manya is heedless with drink. The children, well schooled, brace themselves as the door opens. Blasts of cold followed by blasts of fury make the three of them creep unobtrusively to the farthest corner and huddle together, shivering.

"Byeshintsa!" Sergei screams. "Drunken slut! Gypsy bitch! Pouring money down your filthy gullet." He knocks the bottle

out of Manya's clutch, sending it clattering to the floor. Then he clenches his hand into a fist and drives it into the side of her face.

"Ayieee! Ayieee! Ayieee!" she screams, clutching her jaw and falling to the floor.

He hits her, kicks with his hobnailed boots, landing indiscriminate blows. Manya shrieks, moans, wails, screams, pleads for help. The children hide their faces from the blood and beating but peek up at especially horrific cries, scream in uncontrollable fright. All this commotion is heard by a neighbor, Duvid—the only Jew around.

He comes to the house and, seeing the savagery Manya is enduring, tries to intercede, further enraging Sergei. Plucking up Anna, the littlest, Duvid opens his greatcoat, folds her against his chest and carries her outside.

As the noise inside the house diminishes with distance, his walking takes on a comforting rhythm. She can hear the crunch of his boots on the frozen ground and his thumping chest that pillows her head.

"You will be safe at your grandmother's house," Duvid says, not knowing how to shield her from flying fists and glass without seeming like a busybody. Anna whimpers with fright.

"No one will hurt you there," he says, but her cries of terror escalate as they approach.

"No, no, no!" Anna sobs.

"Too many weeds," Duvid concedes. "Too thick to get in." He carries her to his own house.

Inside, he sets her down on a chair. His wife takes one look at this pale waif, shakes her head and hurries over to the sideboard.

"Eat," she coaxes. She hands Anna a slice of bread spread with a thick layer of strawberry jam.

Anna takes the bread and eyes the mysterious red goo.

"Go ahead. It won't bite," Duvid's wife says, smiling.

Gingerly, Anna lets the tip of her quivering tongue touch the jam. Her large dark eyes grow wide with discovery as she explores the new sensation. While she sits intently devouring the sweet bread, her spindly legs begin to swing, her toes wriggling and squinching with pleasure.

"Look," Duvid's wife says. "No shoes! Bitter cold and no shoes. No meat on her bones. Nothing but a shift and bare feet."

"She doesn't look like them—Manya, Sergei, the other children," Duvid says.

"A different father," says the wife. "Manya claims he died in the war."

"A likely story," Duvid replies, shaking his head. "But what can we do?"

"At least a pair of shoes. See if Leah's old ones fit. In the cupboard by the bed. You get them; I'll give her more jelly bread. It's like she never tasted it before."

"Probably not. Not in that house," says Duvid.

Anna is on the final nub of her second piece of bread when Duvid returns, flustered.

"One shoe is all I found. Three times I looked. I'll look again."

"First see if it fits," the wife says, taking the worn brown leather shoe in her palm and snugging it on Anna's foot. Strained by the events of the day and the concentrated delight of two jelly breads, Anna is mesmerized as she gazes at her one shod foot.

Duvid returns shaking his head. "Just the one." But Anna is oblivious to any lack. She is happily trying every gait possible in her new shoe; heel-toe, trot, hop, skip, slide. One bare foot stands defiantly wedded to the cold earthen floor. The other revels in its small protected world.

"Commotion's over at Manya's," Duvid says. "Better take her back before Sergei makes trouble."

"Faygeleh," says the wife, kissing the top of Anna's head. "You visit again?" Anna nods, speechless and beaming.

Again, Duvid wraps Anna into the warm folds of his great-coat and strides off in the encroaching dark.

For some, home is a place on a road map fixed between rises and curves, canyons and crags, holding fast between the tides. Places like Jackson's Corner, a few houses in a five-dog town, where the world is herded home to snap beans and over-stuffed chairs contoured to familiar shapes. But there were too many blanks in Anna's childhood for home to be charted. In the reeling landscape, she tunes her ear to the hush between Duvid's heartbeats, the quiet between his footsteps—inter-stices that hold time, shape and sound unfurled; the uncreated where all is still possible. It is in this silence that Anna finds a place of peace; the loving sanctuary of a forgotten mother and father; the home she yearns for.

Another time, after her visit to Duvid's house, Anna has an equally magical journey. Wrapped in a blanket and wearing a double layer of Sergei's wool socks, seven-year-old Anna is driven to town to beg for bread while Manya attends to other business. Bordered by towering stands of fir and pine, land and lakes are indistinguishable in the unbroken white. There is a profound hush, except for the soft rustling of the sledge pulled by the family horse over the snow.

Faintly, from far away, a strange melody emerges from the solitude. Movement stirs among the trees, and waving banners appear as a chanting procession winds its way into the open to a glittering object in the distance.

"They are Blessing the Waters," Manya says.

"But everything is ice," Anna says.

"You'll see," replies Manya.

Though the family has been to church only a handful of times, Manya's superstitions and simple, unquestioning religious beliefs reign over many events in their daily life. There is a special shelf jutting out from the timber wall of their izba on which stands a statue of the Virgin Mary. Once, the sun shone in such a way that it appeared the Virgin had a living halo. Neighbors were summoned and were about to send for the clergy to proclaim a miracle, but then the light shifted.

Though Manya, years before, has witnessed Blessing the Waters, the family never has.

At the forefront of the procession, the religious leader, his shoulder-length gray hair meshing with his patriarchal beard, is clad in the violet surplice and cylindrical headdress of the Orthodoxy. After him comes a group of village dignitaries, each bearing a prized icon. Then, following at some distance, come the peasants clad in sheepskin, their wild melody echoing through the woods as they draw closer and closer to a huge cross constructed of blocks of ice.

Manya veers off the barely visible tracks of the road and

maneuvers the sledge toward the gathering. To Anna's amazement, she motions her to dismount. The *batushka*—the
priest—speaks:

"Invisible to our mortal eye, we are followed by a band of
gnomes, sprites, fairies and wood nymphs. As winter approaches, wild creatures draw near to our fires. So too do the
demons of the forest—the Vodiamy, water sprites who love to
make their winter dwellings in the mills and, once there, be-
witch the wooden machinery and cause it to take fire; the
weeping Rousalkas, water nymphs with silvery skin and long
green hair, whose charms lure many a luckless muzhik beneath the shining surface of a lake. Mingled with these are
Liashieë, goat-footed sprites, who delight in luring travelers
into the forest and leaving them there to starve.

"These and others dwell all summer beneath gnarled tree
roots, around the lakes, playing in the rushes and in the green
woodland fields. But now the winter king has come. They are
crushed by his iron hand, and they, like the wolves and foxes,
draw close to the warmth and light of our houses. On this day,
with our chanting and our waving banners, we welcome them
into our midst."

Manya and Anna join as the crowd, still singing, circles
around the glittering cross and looks on as half a dozen peasants with their axes cut a large hole in the ice of the frozen lake
they stand on. The ax strokes ring sharp and clear, like a struck
bell. The singing grows more and more tremulous. All stare intently into the empty circle, for every so often, a human may
glimpse in the dazzle of ice and sun the trembling group of
sprites and gnomes and fairies. The priest's voice intones
words of doom. The spirits must leap into the chasm and sink

far below the surface of the icy water that even now is crusting over. The priest sprinkles holy water upon them as they disappear—the crafty Vodiamy, the treacherous Rousalkas, the cruel Liashieë, and most pitiful of all, the innocent wood nymphs who cannot resist the magic of the potent spell. The priest cannot spare them, for it is impossible to discriminate among the spirit forms. Mothers shield their children's ears, as Manya does Anna's, for it is thought that the young can hear the low, bloodcurdling wail of the innocent wood nymphs.

With the coming of spring, new dangers arise for the peasants. The sprites, free again from their icy prison, seek vengeance. The Church must visit each family in the village and bless every house, barn and field. Although Anna has rarely been inside a church, she is familiar with this spring ritual, especially because the priest, who is recompensed for his blessings at each household with a few kopecks and a glass of vodka, teeters and sways in his duties.

When the ceremony ends, Manya hustles Anna back to the sledge and they continue on to town. But inside Anna, far beneath the stinging tips of her frostbitten aching fingers, something has struck deeply. It leaves her ringing, dazzled, coursing with the same sweet mystery as jelly bread. And most of all wondering. Wondering why these two fleeting moments, tucked in the secret velvet of memory, seem more right, more familiar somehow, than the rest of her life.

Chapter 8

REVELATION

Snow thins to slush. Mud solidifies into summer. Eleven years have passed since Anna came to live with Manya. She is somewhere around thirteen, though she has no idea of when her birthday is. Even if it were known, birthdays are not celebrated in Manya's household. Anna is twiggy as a birch sapling now and just as pale. Her dark eyes, wide with a hunger beyond a full plate, take in all she sees and hears.

She and Olga are seated on the ground outside busily picking off the outer leaves of cabbages for the evening meal and setting aside the hearts. The cabbage hearts will be cut in pieces, placed on the table and chopped with the S-shaped knife with its heavy wooden handle in the middle. The chopped cabbage is packed into casks, sprinkled with salt and pressed down tightly. In a few days, when it bubbles with ferment, the casks will be closed and stored for winter.

"Weed, then ready supper," Manya instructs as she and

Sergei leave for the bazaar in Borschaeevkah to sell three squealing piglets and a crate of pullets.

Olga and Vasil go into the house. Anna, wriggling her toes in the dewy grass, watches the horse cart rumble down the dirt road. Following a snail's wavery glistening trail, she walks to the nearby garden.

Squatting beside a row of cabbages, she tackles a clump of quack grass. She grasps its base, struggling to loosen the deep, mulish roots. Again and again, she repeats the process down the row. Near the last cabbage, she tugs so hard that when the roots finally let go, she loses balance and topples backward. Laughing, Anna sits up and starts to brush the dirt from her shift when she notices a strange man coming down the path to their house. He wears a suit and shoes, nothing like the clothes of local men.

"Hello," he says. "What is your name?"

"Anna Lochotsky," Anna replies, amazed that he would speak to her.

"And where are your parents?" His Russian is stilted and formal, not at all like Chachlatsky, the local dialect.

"Gone to the bazaar."

"Ah," says the man, "that is just as well. You see, they are not really your parents. If you will come with me to your neighbor Duvid's house, I will introduce you to your real grandmother."

"Vasil! Olga!" Anna yells in panic. They come running from the house. "What does this man say? Listen."

"You are not Anna Lochotsky," the man repeats. "You are Anna Axelrood. Your family has been looking for you for a very long time. Your grandmother waits for you now at Duvid's house. Come, child, come with me."

Anna, clutching Vasil with one hand and Olga with the other, begins to cry and shake.

"There, there," says the man, reaching into his pocket and bringing forth a snowy white handkerchief bordered with satin. He dabs Anna's eyes and cheeks and then hands it to her. "For you," he says, his voice calm and gentle. "To keep."

The neatly folded square is as cool and velvety as primrose petals, unlike any fabric she has ever felt. Mesmerized, Anna lets the man lead her, still clutching Olga and Vasil, to Duvid's house.

Approaching the house, they see the back of a woman sitting in a wagon. She is wrapped in a black shawl, and her gray hair is pulled into a bun at the nape of her neck. The particulars of nearness come into focus, the way the color and motion of a sea of wheat articulate into stalks, kernels, sharp whiskers.

The woman turns. She and Anna scrutinize each other intently. The moment stretches out, as slow to thicken as stirred pudding, and then, triggered by who knows what—a shape, a silhouette, an instinct of blood—Anna releases her grip on Vasil and Olga who flank her, and races to the wagon. Leaping up, she and the old woman are in each other's arms, weeping and kissing.

Olga and Vasil watch, stunned, then run off in fright.

Grandma Bessie raises Anna's face and holds it between her wrinkled hands, shaking her head in disbelief. As they look at each other, there is a deluge of more tears, and they bury themselves in each other again. With her nose burrowed into Bessie's ample embrace, and because clothes take up smell and bring back memory more clearly than the mind, Anna is overcome by a deep, wordless recognition of her grandmother.

When their crying finally subsides and Anna slowly raises her face, she sees a group of onlookers gathered around the wagon murmuring in shock. Whispered questions and comments whir about them. Scanning quickly, Anna searches for Olga and Vasil. Nowhere. Guilt and uneasiness are jumbled with her other emotions. She is wrenched by the cost of desire.

"Where's Manya? Sergei?" one of the villagers asks.

Word that they are at the bazaar buzzes from mouth to mouth.

"Someone get her!" yells a man who has more teeth missing than intact.

Grandma Bessie tightens her grip on Anna.

"Come," says the man in the fine suit. "Let us go inside to talk. Duvid will help us translate." He holds out his hand to help the old woman down from the wagon.

Anna jumps down unaided and is quickly enfolded in Grandma Bessie's capacious black shawl. Together, they walk into Duvid's house, Anna measuring her steps to her grandmother's, which are as much side to side as forward.

Duvid holds out a chair for Bessie. Anna sits next to her, Duvid and the suited man across from them. Duvid's wife brings glasses of warm tea for everyone. To Anna, this house is potent with surprise—memories of jelly bread, a shoe and now a grandmother. What other astonishments are being revealed as the fine-suited man speaks to Duvid?

Duvid listens intently to Grandma Bessie, who is talking in some other language that Anna later learns is Yiddish. Turning his full attention to Anna, Duvid leans forward and speaks in his gentle, reassuring voice.

"Anna, you have brothers and sisters who live far away from here in America."

Anna's huge dark eyes are wide with shock. "Olga and Vasil?"

"They are not your true brother and sister, Anna. Really. They are not even related to you."

Again, Grandma Bessie speaks to Duvid, her voice slow and full of emphasis, her hands sculpting the air into something whose weight Anna can feel.

"You have a mother as beautiful as a queen, and a father, who live in America."

"Do you come from America, too?" Anna asks Grandma Bessie.

"No, child, I come from another city in Russia called Kiev," she says, stroking Anna's long dark hair. Her hand comes to rest on the crown of Anna's head, her strong fingers exploring the skull's shape with circular sweeps. Nodding, Bessie's fingertips confirm what her heart already knows. This indeed is her lost granddaughter, the child whose head she caressed and cradled as an infant, learning its intricacies the way lovers learn each other's curves, how they fit in and around each other.

"I have come to take you back, Anneleh. Shoes. You will have shoes." She wipes away tears. "Good food," she says as she kneads the thin stick of Anna's arm. "Good clothes. You'll go to school with other children. Ride trains."

"Trains." Never having seen one, Anna can barely imagine it. "Do I go back to Manya's house now?"

"Only for a short time. Just until we can make a settlement with her. Then you leave forever."

Anna churns with excitement, fear and great sadness at the thought of leaving Olga and Vasil.

Outside, a debate ensues between the neighbors about the propriety of Manya keeping Anna, now the truth is known.

"The thing to do is settle out of court," the man with few teeth says. "Otherwise, Manya will be sent to jail for hiding Anna's true identity."

"Well, what if Manya thought Anna's family was dead?" counters a woman in a flower-print babushka, who is holding the frayed rope of a bleating goat.

"That won't keep Anna from leaving once she's of age," counters another.

"Someone should consult the grandmother, what she intends," says a man, pounding his pitchfork on the ground for emphasis.

"Surely they must pay for eleven years of keeping the child," says the tinker, who goes from village to village selling and sharpening knives and farm tools.

"Look! Here come Manya and Sergei," says someone else. A hush falls.

"Look how swollen and red her eyes are," another whispers.

"She fainted when she heard," says a woman who bustles into the crowd clutching a basket of turnips. "Someone said a woman near Tetiev knows the secret for a long time. Finally, she tells the police, who for years have looked for this lost child."

"I knew something smelled of fish. The child doesn't look like Manya's other ones," snipes a woman, wagging a callused, grimy finger in the air.

A path parts in the crowd as Manya and Sergei make their

way to the house. Negotiations go on through the night into the next day. A price of two thousand rubles is named by Sergei, admittedly high to allow for the well-known Jewish prowess at bargaining.

Finally, it is decided that Grandma Bessie, Anna and Manya ought to go to the nearby town of Berditchev, where Manya will receive her money, the necessary papers will be signed and Anna will then be free to go with her grandmother.

When the door opens and the weary group comes out to the wagon, there is a flurry of commotion. A few neighbors have lingered, coming and going through the night, hoping for further news.

Though Anna has slept the night at Duvid's while the settlement is being worked through, she is bleary with bewilderment. The horse-drawn wagon, driven by the man in the suit, rumbles down the road. Anna's stomach bounces up to her throat with every bump.

Manya will not look at Anna. Her grandmother, who holds her hand tightly in her own, refuses to let go. Anna feels like the quack grass she pulled the day before; uprooted between earth and air with nothing to grasp.

In the heat, clouds of dust swirl up from the horse's hooves as they clop along the sandy ruts of the road. Flies cluster at drops of sweat beading Anna's forehead. Through tangled dark hair, the sun burns into the nape of her neck. She feels woozy as the landscape tumbles and jolts past them. After two hours, they arrive in Berditchev. The cobblestones of the village street rattle every bone in her body.

They climb out of the wagon and enter the low brick courthouse.

"You sit here," the man in the fine suit tells Anna, settling her on a dark wooden bench. At the other end of the room sits an official-looking man in a sheepskin coat decorated with several bronze medals. He is the *starosta,* a quasi-mayor. There is a cacophony of voices from the peasants who wait to go before him to settle disputes over debts, taxes and the division of produce. Anna sits alone, disheveled and frightened. Seeking the comfort of touch, her finger, with its ragged dirty nail, traces around the pocks, nicks and gouges of the old wooden bench.

Papers, talk, pens pass between people; money is exchanged; hands are shaken. When everything is done, the man in the fine suit comes over and, with Grandma Bessie at his side dabbing her leaking eyes, informs Anna that now she is going to leave her foster mother Manya and her brother Vasil and sister Olga and join her real family in America.

Anna weeps.

She does not see Manya leave. She sees only Olga and Vasil, bright as fire, in her mind.

Grandma Bessie gathers Anna's heaving body into her embrace like a bundle of kindling. "Anneleh, Anneleh. So many tears. You and your mama cry so many tears, together you will make an ocean bigger than the one you must cross. Come. Tonight we spend the night with friends. Tomorrow we go on a train to my home in Kiev."

They go to the house of some of Bessie's friends who also were friends of Ben and Lisa and who know the whole bizarre story. When they arrive, people pour from the house to help them from the wagon. Tears, laughter, embraces, a babble of Yiddish. Anna is hugged, wetted by tear-streaked cheeks pressed against hers, rotated around for inspection. They pluck the material of her shift this way and that, furrowing their brows. Pinch the skimpy flesh of her arms and cheeks, shaking their heads in dismay. Push her long dark hair from her face one way, then the other. She is plied with unfamiliar food that she can't eat. There is a radish lodged in her throat; a hard, stinging lump so she can barely swallow.

At length, she is taken to a bed behind a curtain and tucked between sheets that smell of soap. Grandma Bessie, wreathed in smiles, kisses her on the forehead and pats her cheek. "Your first day returned from the dead. Big doings for such a little wisp." Then she disappears into the hubbub on the other side of the curtain.

Anna lies on her back, straight as a corpse, hands balled into white-knuckled fists over her chest. The bed, though small, feels as vast and desolate as the ice-covered span between her old home and the outhouse on a dark winter night. She yearns for the feel of Olga and Vasil next to her, their bodies pressed close to her, their scant body heat mingling until they are as one, warm and breathing, like the newly laid egg Vasil placed in her hand so many years ago. She yearns for the house she knows, its familiar smell of cabbage and bacon grease, its familiar creaks, the snuffling and squawks of the animals outside.

A mother as beautiful as a queen? Trains, oceans, shoes? Tears well up in Anna's eyes, trickle from the corners of her eyes and pool in her ears. Her chest is about to burst, so she turns over to keep her heart from falling out and cries herself to sleep.

She sleeps fitfully and dreams right up to the moment of

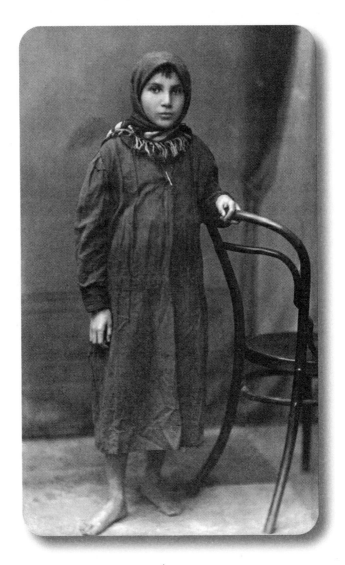

Anna

waking. When she hears stirrings the next morning, she knows that by opening her eyes, she is choosing between worlds— the dark familiar one, and the one that tows her like flotsam to unknown shores. After a breakfast of warm foamy milk and jelly bread, Grandma Bessie takes her (now officially Anna Axelrood) to the railroad station, where they board the train for Kiev. Anna has seen steam snorting from a mare's nostrils on a frosty day, but nothing so huge and raucous and smoke-belching as these trains, big as all the horse carts in Berditchev piled end to end and two high. The hiss and clanks and grind-ing screech send chills laddering up and down her spine. Grandma Bessie, who clasps Anna's hand tightly in her own, feels her shiver, removes her shawl and wraps it around Anna's bony shoulders, frustrated that she didn't have time to get proper clothes and shoes for her before they left.

The steep metal stairs they mount to get into the train are cold and full of strange hard nipples of steel against the soles of Anna's bare feet. They take their seats, Anna next to the window, nose pressed to the glass. The train lurches and be-gins to chug out of the station. Grandma Bessie pats her hand and speaks reassuringly, even though there is little Anna un-derstands.

When they arrive in Kiev, Anna couldn't be more dumb-struck if they had landed on another planet. She feels as if the whole of her is one giant eyeball being imprinted with sight and color and shape. She is awed by everything. Clanging trains race faster than her pounding heart. Her neck hurts from looking up at the tall buildings, so different from the small shacks of Berditchev. Crowds of people are everywhere, dressed in clothes like none she has ever before seen, except for the fine-suited man. They all seem to be staring at her. She pulls Grandma Bessie's black knit shawl more tightly around her potato-sack dress. Before, she never thought about the way she looked. But with no underwear or shoes, a flush of shame burns over her. What monks give up by choice, Anna has achieved by chance, though no sackcloth is as threadbare as the naked heart.

Eefsay, Grandma Bessie's husband, had died a few years before, and Bessie now lives with one of her daughters, Boosie, who is married to the schoolteacher Aaron, and their two sons, Pinucia and Greecha. They are the ones who never left Russia after their failed attempt to cross the Dniester the night the boatman was beaten bloody.

Housing is in extremely short supply. Usually a family of four lives in a single room, sharing a community kitchen and bathroom with other families. Boosie, like all Russian women, works full time. Those with small children arrange for older women to look after them. It is essential that women work to help provide necessities. The boys are in school, but from the time Anna arrives in Kiev until the time she departs for the United States, the Russian government considers her an American. Because of her status as an American, Anna, who never had the opportunity to go to school when she lived with Manya, is not permitted even now to attend public school or to participate in any organized youth activities.

Fortunately, Trania, a cousin who happens to be a retired schoolteacher, offers to tutor Anna while she waits for the passport proceedings to hurdle the respective governments, the biggest problem being no birth certificate, no official document proving her existence. All was lost in Tetiev when their

In her navy sailor dress, Anna works on her lessons.

house burned. Through time and space, the torch of hate, once lit, continues to consume lives.

Affidavits and supporting documents attesting to Anna's birth and family connections have to be gathered from many individuals before the Russian government can recognize her and issue a passport. Furthermore, additional documents have to be obtained from the United States proving that Ben is Anna's father, Lisa her mother, and that Ben once lived in Russia and entered the United States legally.

"China," Trania says, pointing to the map, and painstakingly helps Anna form the letters in her notebook. Nearby is an arithmetic tablet. Anna wipes her hands on the navy sailor dress that replaces her old shift, now cut up into floor rags. She rises early each morning to wash, iron and clean—her contribution to her aunt and uncle for sharing their meager food and space. Anna had just finished scrubbing the floor when Trania arrived, and she does not want any leftover dampness on her hands to blotch the neatly inked words in her workbook.

"Beautiful, Anna," Trania says, smoothing Anna's dark hair. Having no children of her own, Trania has already agreed to let this bright, receptive child come live with her if the government should deny her a passport.

Ten hours a day, six days a week, Trania crams Anna with the world beyond boiled potatoes and rutted mud roads. Anna absorbs the grammar, maps, numbers and ideas as readily as all the praise and attention from Trania. But at night, the ache for Olga and Vasil continues to engulf her. Longing is countered by guilt. She fears that these good people will think her ungrateful for all these opportunities if they see her sad, so she buries her face into her bedclothes and stifles the knots of silent sobs.

But Grandma Bessie knows. "Anneleh, such a sad face," she says, cupping Anna's chin in her hand and looking at her with the acumen of the grocer down the street who can probe deep into the dark brine of the pickle barrel and draw out whatever is called for. "Why are you so sad when you should be dancing for joy to have been found, and to be a human being instead of an animal?

"Look what I bring you from the marketplace," Grandma Bessie tells her. "Ribbon bows for your pretty hair. One for each side." Anna smiles, eyes downcast, embarrassed that her grandma guesses her secret yearnings for the people and places she has left behind.

And at last, one Monday, over a year from the time Anna first came to live with Grandma Bessie, Aunt Boosie, her uncle and cousins, Uncle Aaron comes home from work early. From the pocket of his coat, he ceremoniously withdraws a passport for Anna. Now she can legally depart for America. Brandy is lifted from the high shelf of the mahogany cupboard, and everyone celebrates that Anna will soon be able to join the mother and father who have waited so long.

Everyone except Anna. She looks at the faces of her beloved grandmother and her teacher and once again feels the anchor being wrenched from her gut, about to set her adrift far from all she knows and loves.

The next day, Anna packs her little bag and tearfully hugs her family, especially Trania, good-bye.

At the station, Grandma Bessie lifts Anna's sad face between her wrinkled palms so that their eyes meet. "Please send for me someday. I want to go to America before I die. I want to see my daughter and all my grandchildren. But most of all I want to be with you and see you happy." Their final hug speaks the deep covenant of their blood.

Anna will never see any of these people again.

Chapter 9

JOURNEY OF A

THOUSAND LEAGUES

THE FIRST STOP IS MOSCOW. There government forms and documents have been prepared, executed and stamped. Then off to Germany. In Germany, there are two weeks of delay because of more papers and correspondence between American and Russian authorities to permit passage.

Think, Josh and Jon. It was 1931. The Nazis were already rising in power. By 1935, they had passed the anti-Semitic racial legislation that set the "Final Solution" on its horrific course. Once again, a window of circumstance and history opened just enough for Anna to wriggle through.

From Germany she travels to Riga, in Latvia. "Your passport is not in order," they tell the pale fourteen-year-old when she trudges each day to the HIAS office—the Hebrew Immigration Aid Society, an international organization devoted to helping immigrants. Frightened and lonely, she

СОЮЗ РАДЯНСЬ... ...НИХ РЕСПУБЛІК.

ЗАКОРДОННИЙ ПАШПОРТ.

Пред'явник_ цього, громадянк_ *Украї*
сокої Соціялістичної Радянської
Республіки
і Союзу Радянських Соціялістичних Республік
Аксельрод
Хана Борисівна
виїзджає за кордон СРСР за *Америки*

на посвідчення чого і для вільного виїзду, перебу-
вання за кордоном і поворотного в'їзду до СРСР
видано цей пашпорт з прикладенням печатки.

Цей пашпорт важний для мешкання поза
межами СРСР протягом *Одного*
року з дня переїзду кордону.

Видано *10го Лютого* 1931 року,
в місті *Харкові*

ВІДОМОСТІ ПРО ПРЕД'ЯВНИКА:

Час і місце народження *1917 р. 31. III*
на білоцерковщині
Родинний стан *дівчина*

ПРИКМЕТИ:

Зріст *середній*, Очі *карі*
Ніс *звичайний* Волосся *темне*
Особливі прикмети *нема*

Уповноважений ПКВС УС...
по ... НКВД УС...

Цей пашпорт важний:
для виїзду з СРСР до *10го травня* 1931 р.

СО...
СОВЕТСКИХ СОЦИАЛ...

ЗАГРАНИЧ...

Пред'явительниц...
Социалистическа...
и Союза Советских ...
Акс...
Хана

отправляется за пред...

в удостоверение чего ...
живания за границей...
дан сей паспорт с п...

Настоящий паспор...
ния вне пределов С...
года

Выдан *10го*...
в городе *Харк...*

СВЕДЕНИЯ

Время и место рожд...
Белоц...
Семейное положение ...

П...

Рост *средний*...
Нос *обыкновен...*
Особые приметы *...*

для вы...
через ...

ЮЗ

ТИЧЕСКИХ РЕСПУБЛИК.

ЫЙ ПАСПОРТ.

его, граждан*ка Украинской*
Советской Республики
циалистических Республик

город

Борисовна

ы СССР *в Америку*

ля свободного выезда, про-
обратного в'езда в СССР
ложением печати.

действителен для прожива-
Р в течение *одного*
со дня переезда границы.

февраля 19*31* г.
* же*

ПРЕД'ЯВИТЕЛЬ:

я 1917. 31. III

ковск. окр.

евица

МЕТЫ:

. Глаза *карие*

олосы *шатенка*

ть

Настоящий паспорт действителен
*ка из СССР до 10го мая 19*31* г.
тр.-Погран.-Пропускной Пункт*

UNION
DES RÉPUBLIQUES SOVIÉTISTES SOCIALISTES.

PASSEPORT POUR L'ÉTRANGER.

La porteuse du présent *Axselrod*
Khana
Borissovna
citoyenne de la République Sociale
des Soviets d'Ukraine
et de l'Union des Républiques Soviétistes Socialistes
se rend au delà des frontières de l'URSS *en*
Amérique

en foi de quoi et pour le libre départ, le séjour
à l'étranger et pour le retour dans l'URSS le présent
passeport est délivré avec apposition du sceau.

Le présent passeport est valable pour le séjour hors
des frontières de l'URSS pour la durée de *un*
an à partir du jour où la frontière
a été franchie.

Délivré le *10e Février* 19*31*
à *Kharkoff*

SIGNALEMENT DU PORTEUR:

Lieu et date de naissance *1917. 31. III*
Bielotzerov (gouv.)
État de famille *demoiselle*

SIGNES:

Taille *moyenne* Yeux *bruns*
Nez *ordinaire* Cheveux *chatains*
Signes particuliers *aucun*

Anna has her passport at last.

worries what will happen if she becomes quagmired far from Olga, Vasil, Grandma Bessie, Trania and the mother she doesn't remember. For five weeks, she carries documents, letters, instructions, addresses back and forth to the same officials. Every day the answer is the same.

Where did Anna stay in Riga? With family? With friends? Did the Red Cross or HIAS take care of living arrangements? Neither memory nor records nor any person living can fill in the blanks of who met Anna at each step of the way, where she stayed, how she obtained money for her train tickets and boat passage or any other particulars. All we know is that at last, she is told that her passport is in order and she may resume her trip.

Next stop, France. After two days, she boards a ship to the United States.

If the delay in Riga was rough, the seas were rougher. Anna suffers seasickness throughout the seven-day voyage. She shares a third-class cabin with a woman who speaks only French. When Anna tries to navigate from her cabin to the bathroom, she staggers and weaves like a drunk.

Sympathetic passengers advise her that fresh air is beneficial, so she stumbles aboveboard and grips the railing with whitened knuckles. The water is like churned mercury. From the far horizon, the sun spills over the waves, a long twisting serpent of light. Off the hull of the boat, the scrambling water looks like an infestation of spiders. The sky is full of curdled yellow-gray clouds. Because of her fragile balance, to heave over the side of the ship is precarious, so she lurches below again and stays in her cabin. Lying in her upper bunk, she becomes weaker and weaker, unable to eat or drink.

The small, windowless compartment is like a coffin, and

Anna lies on her back thinking of death. "What will it be like? Will I still miss everyone? Will my guts ever stop churning? Please hurry, let me die."

She feels herself falling down and then a huge jolt. "I must

Anna's "green card" admitting her to the United States.

be dead now," she thinks as she lies unable to move. But she sees the face of the French lady swimming over her. Next comes the face of a man. He raises her arm and holds her wrist between his thumb and forefinger. He examines her and through a translator tells her, "You must eat or you will die. I will send some crackers and lemon water. We have to get you to America, little one, but we can't do that if you don't eat."

Anna is lifted into the lower bunk and falls into a numb sleep. Minutes or hours later—she has no sense of time—the French woman returns and begins to tie something around Anna's neck. Anna doesn't understand what she says but sees she now has a bulb of garlic for a necklace. The woman lifts Anna's head and, breaking a saltine into tiny bits, places them one at a time into her mouth, like the Communion wafers in church the few times Manya took her inside. The task of chewing is arduous; swallowing, an Olympic hurdle; and after a few bites washed down by teaspoons of lemon water, she falls back exhausted.

Somehow Anna survives the passage and, though unsteady and as thin as the ship's railing, readies herself as the boat docks in New York. She pulls out the picture of her mother and father from her packet of documents and sits on the bunk waiting for them to come and get her. Three strangers appear, a man and two women. Anna is confused and frightened.

They hug her and pick up her small suitcase to leave. Anna looks from the photograph to the strangers and back to the photograph.

"No," she says as adamantly as her reedy strength can muster. She speaks in Yiddish. "You are not my parents."

"That's right," Uncle Mike replies in Yiddish. "I am Uncle

"I am Uncle Mike. This is your aunt Sophie."

Mike, this is your aunt Sophie, and this is Rae, your sister, who lives with us while she goes to school in New York."

Anna looks from Mike, who has the sensitive face and eyes of a poet, to beautiful Sophie, stern and daunting as a school-marm, to Rae.

"But my parents say America, I come, they come. I wait."

Uncle Mike stoops down on one knee by Anna and pats her hand. "America is a very big country, Anneleh. Your parents live all the way in Chicago, Illinois. Nine hundred miles away. That's where all your other brothers and sister live, too—Jean, Morrie, Jackie and little Seymour. First you come home with us for a few days. Then you go on a train to Chicago. That's when your mother and father will meet you."

The ship's doctor, who has come into the cabin, interrupts. "Excuse me. I'm sorry, but I cannot permit this child to leave. She is little more than walking death. Moving her at this time would be far too risky. Tomorrow, perhaps."

"Tomorrow, then," says Uncle Mike, standing to kiss Anna on the top of her head. Aunt Sophie and Rae place a kiss on each of Anna's cheeks and depart.

All the way back to Long Island, they talk of nothing but the pathetic state of Anna.

You must think I'm embellishing, Josh and Jon, adding dramatic delay to ante the emotional stakes, but I'm not. This is life, not art. There are no book covers to close between chapters, no riding off into sunsets, no harmonic resolutions. In life, it seems we always are waiting for something—pay-checks, picket fences, dreams come true. Primed like run-ners, we race toward the goal of the day, dumbfounded when it turns out to be a Sisyphean marathon.

.   .   .

When Uncle Mike, Aunt Sophie and Rae arrive back home in Long Island, Jesse, their son, is beside himself. "Papa," he says, shoving his thick glasses back up his nose, "someone has stolen two dollars from my drawer."

Uncle Mike, always the peacemaker, asks, "Boychik, are you sure somewhere else you didn't put it?"

"I'm sure, Papa."

"We ask then. Money doesn't grow on trees. Neither does it disappear into thin air," says Mike, who knows this well. He is a machine shop foreman for the IRT and brings in a bare-bones salary even though he is a mechanical genius, writing many articles for *Popular Mechanics* and inventing a number of things that, had he patented them, would have made him a rich man.

"Frances, Ann. Come in here. Do either of you know what happens to your brother's two dollars?"

"No, Papa," says seven-year-old Frances, shaking her bobbed head emphatically.

"Me neither." Ann, who is ten, looks down at her feet.

Uncle Mike, hand in his pants pocket, jiggles coins, shifting pennies as rapidly as thoughts.

"Hmmm . . . ," he says to Ann. "Stick out your tongue, girlie."

Ann does. It is red.

"This tongue of yours, it gets red with too much sun?"

"No, Papa. Candy."

"Candy. So. And where does this candy come from? Not your mother. Of this I'm sure. Jesse, Frannie, you can go now back to your business. So, Ann, you were about to tell from where this candy comes."

"Oh, Papa," cries Ann. "It was me. I took Jesse's money to buy candy for the girls at school so they will like me."

"I see. Girlie, let me tell you something. If they can't see enough to like without candy, then you don't want them for friends anyway. Now we must think what to do. This is serious business, girlie. Taking money from your brother."

"Yes, Papa," Ann says, her beautiful fine features tearstained.

"I'm going to have to spank you."

Ann is shocked. Never in her life has her father lifted a hand to her unless to pat a cheek or give a hug.

After several hard whacks on her bottom, Uncle Mike says, "Now I am going to have to spank you again. Before, I spanked you because you lied. Now I spank you because you stole." After several more whacks, he takes Ann into his arms and hugs her. "No more stealing, no more lying?"

"No, Papa," Ann says, crying.

"Good. It hurt me more than it hurt you, girlie," he says, wiping her tears. "Only in a different place."

I wonder if Mike and Sophie had qualms about childrearing? Since your birth, Josh and Jon, theories on the do's and don'ts of parenting are like a game of in-and-out-the-window. Spank, and you teach your child physical abuse (and besides, it doesn't work). Don't spank, and you spoil the child. Time-outs, lost privileges, the psychology of raising a hand or raising a voice left me punishing myself for not knowing the right thing to do. I made so many mistakes, illumined now in the glare of hindsight.

Every time you passed each other, you would heckle or

poke a playful jab. Why didn't the truth of all those nature programs smite me where it counted—lions, bears and wolf cubs cuffing each other in mock fight? I should have seen that the animal was alive and well. Later, you channeled testosterone into arm wrestling. And now, as you go your own directions, it amuses me that within a few hours of reuniting, guttural bellows and musk fill the air as you challenge each other once again. Are you testing family standing? Who is the force to be reckoned with?

What can we say for sure about raising kids anyway? Kids grow like plants; some need more care than others. Direct light for one might wither another. The rich soil of a violet would kill a cactus. Some like space, others to be rootbound.

Parents like Mike, like Lisa, have green thumbs. Others, like me, worry themselves into a frazzle, when in the long run, I wish I could have fretted less and enjoyed more. Spent my seconds fully present, not second-guessing.

Years later, Frances recalls another example of her beloved father Mike, in 1944, when she was twenty.

"When I got married, my mother, Sophie, was not happy with my choice. She wouldn't come to the wedding, and she was furious because my father did. When he wanted to buy me a wedding present, he didn't have any money because he turned his check over to Sophie and she allotted him only enough for carfare.

"My brother, Jesse, had very bad eyesight, and that's why he couldn't go into the armed forces. He went to a plant at night that made radios for the war effort. He used to sit at a table and take the rubber off wires, which were made into radio parts. My father, a gray-haired balding man, shleps into the plant, hand in his pocket jiggling his money, and asks for the manager. He says, 'Hi, I'm Mike Axler.'" The clerk at Ellis Island had shortened the family name when he came to America. " 'I have a son who works here. I'll go around this place for a half an hour, you give me fifty dollars, and I'll tell you how to improve it.'

"The guy says, 'Who are you? What do you mean, fifty dollars? What are you talking about?'

"Mike says, 'I'll go around, tell you how to improve it.'

"So the guy is making millions, they were making millions during the war, he thinks Pop is meshuggener, but he'll give him fifty bucks. He says, 'Okay.'

"So Pop walks around, he sees what they're doing, he watches Jesse. Jesse's knife becomes dull, he goes over to a pumice stone, sharpens the knife, comes back, takes the rubber off the wire.

"Then Pop says, 'Boychik, get up, get up.' Jesse gets up. Pop sits down, he measures, he looks at the table, he says, 'Okay, sit down.' He says to the manager, 'Okay, you got to give me twenty-eight dollars and fifty cents more.'

"The manager says, 'You said fifty dollars!'

" 'Fifty dollars is for me. Twenty-eight fifty is for the parts. I'll be back next week.'

" 'But you were only here twenty minutes!'

" 'I was here long enough.'

"So the manager gives him seventy-eight dollars and fifty cents and the next week my father comes back, goes over to the table and says, 'Boychik, get up.' Jesse gets up. My father has a case full of tools. He cuts a hole in the table with a saw.

"The manager protests, 'What are you doing!'

" 'Everything's going to be all right,' says Mike. 'Don't worry.'

"In the hole he has cut, he attaches a small pumice stone that is flush with the table. Underneath it, he attaches a small motor, connected to the pumice stone, which is now turning.

"He says, 'Boychik, sit down. Do your job.'

"Jesse puts the wire on the pumice stone, touches his knife to it, and the rubber flies off. Jesse does ten wires in the time it takes the other men to do one.

"The manager says, 'Listen, you come back next week for half an hour, I'll give you a hundred dollars, anything you want.'

"Papa says, 'I needed fifty dollars, thank you very much, good-bye.'

"He bought me a Beautyrest bed for my wedding present," Frances finishes. "We slept on it for fifteen years."

That was Mike Axler.

The next day, Uncle Mike returns to the ship to get Anna. He misses a second day of work with no pay. On a pittance salary and with three children to raise, this means Sophie's meager budget will grow even tighter, her stew soupier. But everyone is far too full of anticipation to care.

The ship's doctor takes him aside and advises him of the precariousness of Anna's condition, how close she has been to death and still is, that she needs time to build strength and stamina. Finally, he releases her to Mike.

By the time they arrive on Long Island, where Uncle Mike and Aunt Sophie live with their three children, Anna is exhausted and ill. Even though Mike and Sophie are poor by

American yardsticks, their house seems like a mansion to her; the simplest food a feast.

There are many people waiting there, all excited to greet her: impulsive Uncle Robert, the youngest of the Axelroods (the one who saved his papa, Shimin, from hanging) and his family; his wife Rose, who had traveled from New York to Washington in order to search for Anna through the Red Cross and HIAS; friends and neighbors.

Anna is so weak she can barely walk and understands only a few splinters of English. They all stare at this apparition. She weighs less than eighty pounds and is the color of pale yellow wax. Questions and comments swarm around and at her. She sees their pitying stares and once again feels the encumbrance of a physical body. She longs for her faceless times with Olga and Vasil, when life was so permeable that they were one. It is a relief when everyone leaves.

Before bed, Rae (who at twenty-six is the oldest of Ben and Lisa's children) takes her newly returned sister to the bathroom, plunks her into a steaming tub and administers, as only Rae can, a scrubbing that turns Anna's antique yellow to red, then to black and blue. The next morning, Aunt Sophie takes one look at this skeletal, bruised waif and, stiffening her already ramrod posture, declares, "Anneleh. Here you are going to stay until I fatten you up a little. Your mother, who waits all these years for you, shouldn't see you like this."

"Aunt Sophie, tomorrow we're to put her on the train," Rae says.

"Look at her," Sophie whispers. "To send her off like this would be wrong. Fatal even. Maybe a week, week and a half. No more discussion. I have decided."

Sophie sits Anna on a stool in the kitchen to keep an eye on her, gives her a piece of white bread with butter on it and begins to cook.

"Cake?" Anna asks, biting into the first non-brown bread she has tasted.

First Sophie makes a big pan of kasha varnitshkes. As she minces onion, it is not Sophie but Anna who sheds tears. She browns the onions in chicken fat, more than the usual third-cupful, hoping it will change from chicken fat to Anna fat. She combines cooked kasha with boiled noodles, salts, peppers, sprinkles it liberally with grebenes (bits of chicken skin fried crisp) and plunks a plate of this on the counter in front of Anna. Sophie scrapes the remaining kasha onto a plate, running the spoon round and round the seemingly empty pan with the care of one who knows that little specks add up—add up to another head of wheat that had to be sown, grown, harvested, threshed, milled, sacked, hauled, bought, mixed, cooked and served. There was too much work, too much life in the tip of the spoon, to be lost down the drain.

"Eat!" says Sophie. "And when you are full, eat more. We have to get some meat on these chicken bones of yours." Then she proceeds to bake the challah bread and a sponge cake for the Sabbath meal. Before she slips the cake into the oven, she puts the mixing bowl in front of Anna.

"Lick," she says, also handing her the beater thick with batter.

Anna's shrunken stomach resists the richness and quantity of food, but once Sophie has made up her mind about something, there are no chinks left for argument. If the Angel of Death passed over Anna in Russia, in Germany, in the middle of the Atlantic Ocean, it surely is not welcome here. Not in Sophie's household. Anna will get better and Sophie will see to it, no two ways about it.

Outside, thunder begins to crash, and a downpour pelts the roof.

"Acchh! It rains," says Sophie, brushing back a dark wave from her forehead. "Now people will bring mud into my clean house." But Anna does not hear. At the first flash of light, she bolts from her stool, grabs several cups from the kitchen sink, fills them with water and runs around like a wild person placing them on every windowsill. Ashtrays, saucers, bowls, any vessel she can lay her hands on is snatched up, until she's certain every window has its own container of water on the sill to catch the lightning.

"Mama, what's she doing?" whispers Frances, wide-eyed.

"Must be some crazy idea. Something from before, when she lived with that gypsy woman. Don't pay no mind. You worry about you. Are you finished polishing furniture?"

"Almost. I just have the dresser in your room," says Frances.

"What goes on? You been up there a long time."

"Frannie was showing us something, that's why," Jesse says, coming in to put the broom away.

"Showing what?" Sophie asks, her high-arched eyebrows lowering into shelves of suspicion.

"How the top of the bedpost lifts off and makes a secret hole where you hide your Sabbath pearls."

Sophie screeches, grabs the broom from him and starts to chase Frances around the house. "*Ich gay trayten oft der mit mein fees!* I'll stomp you with my feet!"

Even though there's a storm, Frances heads for the door. She flings it open, poised to tear outside, and bumps into her father. Mike catches her and holds her in his soggy embrace.

"Papa! Papa! Mama says she's going to stomp me!" Sophie rounds the corner of the hallway in hot pursuit, still wielding the broom.

"Sophie, Sophie!" Mike says. "What could be so bad?"

"You make puddles on my clean floors, the whole world should know where I keep my pearls, Anneleh acts like a crazy person and now my food burns. *Bad?*"

"You go cook," Mike says masterfully, shifting Frances behind him. "Everything else, I will do."

The storm abates, Sophie calms down and ten more days pass. Sophie's regimen works. By the time Anna boards the train for Chicago, she has gained weight and feels much better.

The bustle of Grand Central Station adds to the hubbub of all the relatives and friends who accompany her there. Anna has never seen anything so vast, so full of hurrying people. It is the first time she has ever seen a black person, even though she has read about them, and she is fascinated. When she boards the train, Uncle Mike gives some money to the darkest man she has ever seen.

"You take good care of her," he says. "See she has food, something to drink, and gets off here." He points to her ticket. "See you this fall, girlie. When we come for the bar mitzvah of Seymour-Uncle-Itzzy's." (So dubbed to distinguish him from the other Seymour in the family.) Gently he kisses her on her forehead.

"Yes sir, I will. I'll take good care of this little miss," the porter assures him.

This is somewhat difficult because Anna speaks little English and the porter speaks no Russian. So they speak with their hands, the language of dancers, babies, lovers and those who cannot hear.

The porter brings her food and drink. He covers her with a blanket when she falls asleep at night, but every time the train stops, Anna gets up and puts on her coat—actually one that was Jesse's, which replaced the shabby, leaden, oversize one that had been passed on to her in Kiev.

"No, not yet, little miss," the porter tells her each time. "You come on back and sit down. I'll let you know when it's your stop. You can be sure of that."

But the next time the train stops, Anna again jackrabbits out of her seat and starts to leave. "This time it must be stopping for me," she thinks.

Again the porter guides her back. "You're goin' to hop off into the wrong state to the wrong mama and daddy if you don't sit yourself down till I tell you," he says, laughing.

Anna wonders if her whole life is one long trip without ever getting to where she's supposed to be. Outside the window, scenery speeds by in a blur. From the glass she sees the faces of Olga and Vasil staring at her, the faces of Trania, Grandma Bessie, disjointed scenes of people and places all jumbled together. The hypnotic chug of the train repeats her despair over and over.

At last, the friendly porter appears, brushes off her coat, gathers up her bag and leads her to the exit door.

The train stops, and she starts down the steps. A woman's piercing shrieks almost deafen her. Someone grabs her and lifts her off her feet. A huge crowd shouts and jockeys for position. Out of the pandemonium, the woman continues to scream as if she is being stabbed. The man who is carrying her in his shaking arms is crying.

"This must be my father, my mother," Anna realizes. In the picture, they look younger. Photographers' bulbs flare. Bright bubbles of light obscure the faces of all the people who press toward her. A band begins to play. The Boy Scouts are there. The mayor is there. Banners wave—"Welcome home Anna." Someone thrusts a basket of flowers into her hand as Ben carries her to Lisa, who keeps screaming over and over, unable to stanch the flood of twelve years of worry, fear, anguish, grief and hope.

"Anneleh, Anneleh, Anneleh," she sobs, clutching her.

"Mameh?" Anna whispers.

As Ben puts Anna down, two of her brothers, Seymour, aged four, and Jack, aged nine, are shoved forward by her twenty-year-old sister, Jean.

Jack, in a suit and necktie, maintains the solemn demeanor befitting a boy who has graduated to long pants. Seymour reaches up to hand his new sister a flower.

Again flashbulbs crackle. The next day, a picture of them appears in the *Chicago Daily News*. Saturday, April 11, 1931.

LOST AS BABY, GIRL REJOINS PARENTS HERE.

Lost as a baby twelve years ago, when her parents fled before Bolshevist raiders from the burning

LOST AS BABY, GIRL REJOINS PARENTS HERE

Anna, Now 14, Was Separated by Red Raid on Town in 1919.

Lost as a baby twelve years ago, when her parents fled before bolshevist raiders from the burning town of Tetiev, in soviet Russia, Anna Axelrood, now 14 years old, arrived here last night after a lone journey from Europe to rejoin her newly found family. She was greeted in the Union station by her parents, Mr. and Mrs. Benjamin Axelrood of 454 Roslyn place, and a large group of friends.

Anna was a baby of 2, youngest of four children, when the village of Tetiev was destroyed in 1919. As the terrorized townspeople fled from the soldiers the members of the Axelrood family were separated and Anna was carried off by a peasant woman who found her in a field near Tetiev.

Axelrood and his wife were reunited a few days later with three of their children in the city of Kiev. They went to Rotimania, meanwhile continuing a search for Anna. Then they moved to Chicago. For the last ten years the towns and farms around Tetiev were combed by friends of the Axelroods in an attempt to find the girl.

Last year a peasant woman disclosed to neighbors in Tetiev that she had been guardian of a secret since 1919, that a girl growing up on a near-by farm was really the lost Anna. The police investigated, verified the story and compelled the guardians by court order to turn over Anna to her Chicago parents.

The girl then began the journey alone to meet her father and mother, whose faces she could not even vaguely remember. When she got off the train here last night the parents embraced her.

Axelrood is the owner of a laundry at 1125 Rush street.

HAPPINESS REIGNS AGAIN!

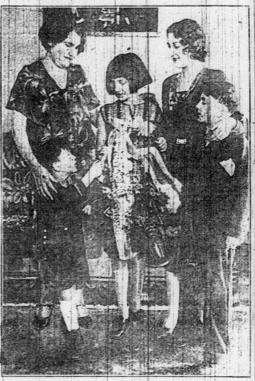

Anna Axelrood, 14 years old, is a happy girl today, for after being lost from her family since a bolshevist raid on the village of Tetiev, soviet Russia, in 1919, she was reunited last night after a trip from Russia alone. She is shown between her mother, Mrs. Lena Axelrood, and her 19-year-old sister, Jean, at their home at 454 Roslyn place, this morning. In front are Anna's two brothers, Seymore, 4 years old, and Jack, 9.
[By a staff photographer.]

AUTOIST HELD TO JURY IN DEATH OF BOY, 4

Stanley Stepancevitch of Hammond, Ind., was held to the grand jury on a charge of manslaughter by a coroner's jury at an inquest into the death of George Lique, 4 years old, 4131 Wallace street, who was killed when the

MRS. KASPAR SCHMIDT TO GET HER DIVORCE

The question of whether four or five glasses of beer constitute the violation of a husband's promise to his wife to stay on the water wagon featured the renewed divorce suit of town of Tetiev, in Soviet Russia, Anna Axelrood, now 14 years old, arrived here last night after a lone journey from Europe to rejoin her newly found family. She was greeted in the Union station by her parents, Mr. and Mrs. Benjamin Axelrood of 454 Roslyn Place, and a large group of friends.

Anna was a baby of 2, youngest of four children, when the village of Tetiev was destroyed in 1919. As the terrorized townspeople fled from the soldiers, the members of the Axelrood family were separated and Anna was carried off by a peasant woman who found her in a field near Tetiev. Axelrood and his wife were reunited a few days later with three of their children in the city of Kiev. They went to Roumania, meanwhile continuing a search for Anna. Then they moved to Chicago. For the last ten years the towns and farms around Tetiev were combed by friends of the Axelroods in an attempt to find the girl. Last year a peasant woman disclosed to neighbors in Tetiev that she had been guardian of a secret since 1919, that a girl growing up on a near-by farm was really the lost Anna. The police investigated, verified the story and compelled the guardians by court order to turn over Anna to her Chicago parents.

The girl then began the journey alone to meet her father and mother, whose faces she could not even vaguely remember. When she got off the train here last night the parents embraced her.

Axelrood is the owner of a laundry at 1125 Rush Street.

According to the *News,* Lisa is spared twenty-eight vermin-infested days in Yossip's attic mourning her baby. Anna's year and a half of waiting, journeys, adjustments, despair and near-death are erased. Even the street name is wrong.

In a way, Josh and Jonny, I guess it's not so dire. Time and memory do this to us all. Things we know fog and recede. Other memories, knowledge from the collective conscious and unconscious, seep like groundwater into our brain. Always, biology and instinct burble beneath the surface.

Yet something equally mysterious and unpredictable is at work, too. Something woven into every worm and rock, into wind and water and fingernail parings; something that makes dung as sacred as prayer. Something we call God.

Stunned, Anna arrives at 454 Roslyn Place, the new apartment that, only a year before, Ben and Lisa moved into from the back of their laundry.

Quickly, the place fills with people. Food lines the tables and counters, with new bowls and platters accompanying each wave of visitors. Everyone talks at the same time. Anna is passed through a gauntlet of love. She is overwhelmed by the din, by a barrage of language she can't understand and the emotional tempest swirling about her.

At last, all the well-wishers leave.

That night, as she tucks Anna under the sheets, Lisa sits on the edge of the bed and lovingly traces her child's features. Anna's dark eyebrows, her pale veined eyelids. Her anemic lips and cheeks, so much longer and thinner than the rounded curves Lisa's hand remembers. There is a twelve-year hole in their lives together that Lisa's hand must stretch to cover.

The onslaught of Anna's new life begins. A new bed, new family, new home, new people, new language, new customs. Added to the hectic routine of home life, a series of weekly banquets in her honor is hosted by various organizations. She is woodpeckered with questions. "*Vee gehfelt ihn Ahmehreekah? How do you like America?*" everyone keeps asking.

At fourteen, she enters grade school in a class of young children, struggling to catch up with her peers and to master the language. She endures the taunts of other children because of her accent, though eventually, through practice and the help of a friend who teaches her diction with the aid of a mirror to illustrate tongue placement, she comes to speak English without a trace of Russian accent. In only four years, she will complete grade school with top honors, graduating in the same class as her little brother Jackie.

Years later, Anna marries and, according to her middle child, Bruce (as well as all who know her), is devoted to her family, loves to laugh, has no hint of melancholy and appreciates even the simplest pleasures in life.

And only occasionally does she dream in terror of Grandmother Lochotsky's dark, smoky hut.

Chapter 10

FORKS AND SHOES

S EPTEMBER 1931. Indian summer is upon Chicago, graced by the season's last flowers: roadside chicory and Queen Anne's lace, priapic red sumac, delicate pastel sweet peas and blazing chrysanthemums. Leaves begin to tinge and whisper secrets to the air.

Everyone gets ready for the bar mitzvah of Seymour-Uncle-Itzzy's. He is the son of Uncle Itzzy—Irving—the fourth-born son of Shimin and Chana. All the relatives from New York will arrive in Chicago this evening in anticipation of tomorrow's ceremony.

In Ben and Lisa's laundry on State Street, Lisa gets up from the sewing machine where from early morning until nine each night she mends loose buttons, socks, ripped bedsheets, undershirt holes and BVDs and reverses shirt collars and cuffs free of charge as part of the service. She takes a clean laundry bag, unfurls it over the table for a cloth and begins preparations for the family's dinner. With fourteen- to fifteen-hour

Lisa, Jack and Ben are behind the counter of the laundry.

workdays, almost all of the family's life, except for sleeping, takes place in the back of the laundry. As she slices potatoes, she sings a Russian song, something she does only in private, her voice a rich coloratura, warbling and pure as Jenny Lind's. As the door opens and shuts, she snaps to attention; force of habit for someone who has lived in a time and place where uninvited strangers entered with guns and loved ones left and disappeared.

Anna, who has been in America a little over five months, comes in carrying her books strapped together and lays them on the counter.

"So Anneleh," Lisa says, reverently placing her hand on the books, "tell me what you learn today?"

"Words with O," Anna says. "When teacher talks 'ocean,' I feel sick, like to throw up. I learn all 'bout ocean already." They laugh.

"Here, have a little snack before you go up front," Lisa says, squeezing her shoulder. "Don't forget, today Sylvia comes over special to take you to the store for new shoes for the bar mitzvah."

"Bought shoes," Anna says excitedly.

"Where's Jackie?" Lisa asks, wiping her hands on her apron.

"He walk behind," Anna says, grabbing an apple and leaving the steamy back room, smelling of soap, wet clothes and borscht, to go help her twenty-year-old sister Jean, at the front desk. Jean loves to mother Anna and, between customers, helps her with homework every day.

In a crib in the corner of the back room, pudgy little Seymour wakes up from his nap and sits like a dazed puppy.

"Come on, sleepyhead, Mameh's going to get for you some milk. Then you sit here and I get brown wrapping paper and you make for your papa a nice picture."

Ben comes in looking tired.

"Ben, Ben, come sit down," Lisa says, pulling out a chair. "Again, you overdo."

It is only a year since Ben's operation. Two years ago nagging back pain was diagnosed as kidney deterioration. Last year, in 1930, he underwent surgery for removal of a kidney, a very hazardous procedure for the times, usually with a bleak outcome.

But Ben, who had made the sky bend before to safekeep his Lisa before she left for Cherepin to search for Anna, did so again; this time to preserve himself for Anna's long-waited-for arrival.

Lisa brings him a glass of water. "Drink," she says, going back to the stove to stir.

"Where's Jackie?" Ben looks at the stack of string-tied brown-paper parcels waiting to be delivered.

"Anna says he comes. But so far, no."

Ben gulps down the water and hauls himself up. He leafs through the tickets on several bundles.

"Achh, this one goes to der toyber, the deaf one," says Ben, who has a name for everyone. "This one to der missickener, the terrible one. And this one to der yenta, the gossip."

He selects several and pecks his wife on the cheek, letting his free hand slide over her breast.

"Ben!" she admonishes him lovingly, inclining her head sharply toward Seymour.

"Good he should learn early," Ben says, grinning. As he passes by his son, who sits on the floor coloring, Ben kisses his fingertips and places them on the top of Seymour's head, the same way the mezuzah on the doorpost of a Jewish home is kissed as a blessing upon entering or exiting.

Lisa smiles and begins the dough for the liver-filled knishes; some for tonight, some to bring to the bar mitzvah meal tomorrow. For the filling, she peels an onion. Tears stream down her cheeks as she chops through layers, concentric as the growth rings of a tree—tiny pieces, shards, all those years heaped in a crystalline pile. And though she is content, her ankle still has a weeping ulcer, as if the news that Anna is found hasn't gotten all the way down to her foot.

She makes extra food for the arrival from New York of

Mike's family late tonight, chuckling at the thought of Sophie, Mike and their three children—Ann, Frances and Jesse—in their old Model T. Uncle Mike is able to tinker any problems in the old car back into working condition, and frugal Sophie, well aware of the expense of feeding a family of five on a nine-hundred-mile trip, always ties to the side of the car a five-pound salami and a four-pound loaf of pumpernickel. Whenever anyone is hungry, she hacks off a chunk from each. And so the journey goes, the oily reek of garlic turning the heads of gas station attendants, pedestrians and other motorists as their mobile deli passes.

Ben returns for more deliveries and sees the stack the same height as when he left. "Still no Jackie!"

Lisa dips a long-handled spoon into the borscht and beckons Ben to come taste. As he blows on it, nine-year-old Jack sneaks in the door, pants dirty from playing ball, and quietly takes a bundle from the stack, hoping his father, whose back is turned, will think he's been delivering all afternoon and come back for more.

"Der he is," Seymour says, pointing his chubby finger.

Ben wheels around. "*Shtick flaysh*—you piece of meat! *Zollst brennen ahf goz und zoll fin dir nisht bleibin kein schooreh de poorerch*—may you burn like gauze and may there not remain any dust or ash!"

Jack retreats until his back is pressed against the wall as Ben advances, wielding his forefinger like an ax with every word.

Lisa, wiping her hands on her apron, quickly grabs an armful of bundles, thrusts them at Jack and shoves him out the door.

"Soon Mike and Sophie will be here. Better finish with the deliveries," she says, rapidly patting Ben's back as if she were burping an infant. "The soup. Is all right? Maybe needs more salt?"

"Soup's fine," Ben grumbles. "Don't worry about dessert, because I'm going to make baked apple out of that little scoundrel."

"Ben, Ben, it's no good to get your blood worked up. Let it go."

"Is true," he says, sighing heavily. "It's a burden to carry, but a pity to throw away." Lisa detects the sliver of a twinkle in his eye as he takes an armful of deliveries and leaves.

"Mameh," Anna says, coming into the back room breathless with excitement, "Sylvia here."

"Sister, Sister—just who I need," Lisa says. "Come taste. Nobody makes borscht like your papa, Morris." She stirs the pot, dips and holds it out for Sylvia's approval. "Careful, don't burn your tongue," she says as Sylvia blows, takes a tentative sip, works it around her tongue, swallows and finishes with several contemplative smacks of her lips. "So . . . ?"

"Nothing," Sylvia pronounces. "Good as Papa's."

"You don't think a little more sugar?"

"Tastes perfect to me, Aunt Lisa."

"Then I leave it alone. Now. About the shoes. Size, I don't know. Always she has shoes handed down, handed up, handed over, or no shoes. You make sure there's plenty room in the toes for her to grow."

"I will, Aunt Lisa. I'll have the salesman measure twice."

"Something sturdy, but something pretty. She gets to be a young lady like you, Sister."

"Yes, Aunt Lisa." Sylvia, sixteen, two years older than Anna, flashes a smile to her.

Lisa fishes in her pocket and brings out a tight roll of bills. "Here, take."

"No, no. Papa says he pays."

"To your papa we owe too much thanks already. Take."

"I can't, Aunt Lisa. Papa insists. He says it's his pleasure."

"What can I say but thank you? He's a good man, Morris, your papa. Go now. Aunt Sophie and Uncle Mike will be arriving tonight." Lisa has spread three crackers with some of the mashed chicken-liver filling for the knishes. "Here," she says, giving one to Anna and one to Sylvia. She gives another to Anna. "Take this out to your sister Jean before you go."

"Yes, Mameh."

"Thank you, Aunt Lisa," Sylvia says, daintily licking the remains from her fingertips.

"Jackie, he come?" Anna asks.

"Yes, but that's another story. Go now. Seymour, say good-bye to Anneleh and Sister." Seymour looks up from his drawing and waves amiably.

"Come, bubbelah. Help Mameh set the table. You count out forks and spoons," she says.

Seymour drags a chair over, climbs onto it and stands in front of the utensil drawer.

"Such a big boy," Lisa says, opening the drawer. She goes back to rolling and filling knishes.

Seymour takes out a fork and places it on the counter. "One for me. One for Papa. One for Mameh. One for brudder Jackie. One for thithter Jean. One for thithter Anna. One for brudder Morrie. One for thithter Rae. One for me."

"Already you did 'one for you,' bubbelah. Now count up and see how many that makes."

"One, two, free, four . . ."

Lisa is unsure which gives her more pleasure: hearing Seymour increase in skills or hearing the names of all her family, counted out together to rub elbows at the same table.

"Now count out spoons, bubbelah," she says, slipping a cookie sheet dotted with half-moon knishes into the oven.

A while later, the table is set for the Sabbath meal, and the smell of good things to eat in the steam-laden room is soup for the nose. Anna and Sylvia come in bustling with excitement. Anna carries a bag clutched to her chest.

"We found good shoes, Aunt Lisa. Anna tried them on and decided these were the ones. They fit just like you want. But when the clerk took them away to wrap, Anna got very upset. She didn't understand she would get them back."

"Ohh," Lisa says, patting Anna's cheek in sympathy. "Show, show." Anna starts to unwrap them.

"We can always take them back if you don't approve, Aunt Lisa," Sylvia says.

"Don't approve?" Lisa says, clasping both hands together at her bosom and beaming as Anna spins around and around modeling the black-patent-leather pumps with their delicate T-strap. "So beautiful. Look, Seymour, your sister, a shayne maidel, a shayne maidel. Thank you, Sister." She goes to Sylvia and, holding her face between her hands, kisses each cheek alternately over and over. "Tomorrow I thank your papa myself. Today you take this. Here, let me wrap," she says, plucking knishes from the tray and placing them on brown paper. She ties them into a neat bundle with string and presses it into Sylvia's hands. "Thank you, Sister. At the bar mitzvah we see you, okay?"

"Good-bye, Aunt Lisa, Anna, Seymour. See you tomor-row," Sylvia says, smiling her dimpled smile, her blue eyes dancing.

Almost forty years later, I can still remember my bas mitzvah. Two years of Hebrew school; contemplating the topic I would speak on related to my Torah portion; Mother baking and freezing cookies months in advance (my favorite was a buttery confection the size of a half dollar with a chocolate mint wafer hidden inside); buying the brown scoop-necked dress with its bolero jacket; trying to cover my pimples with makeup; listening carefully to my brother sing a special solo from the pulpit so I could yardstick my nervousness to his, because throughout my childhood he was the forward scout to warn of what lay ahead; the kindly wise eyes of the rabbi as he handed me the silver pointer to read the words in the Torah so my hands wouldn't touch the sacred scrolls.

Though you are both of Jewish blood, Josh and Jonny, you have little firsthand knowledge of bar mitzvahs. Jonny, you did go to a friend's once; an unforgettable experience, as much for what preceded it as the event itself. Dad was out of town, and not used to dressing up, you borrowed a tie from his closet. The problem then became how to tie it. Since none of our neighbors was home and time was short, you were both mortified and amused when I dragged you out to the sidewalk and nabbed the first man who walked by, assured him that this was not *Candid Camera* and asked for help.

Dad and I did attempt to create meaningful rites of passage. When you turned eighteen, Josh, we went down by the creek and had a ceremony. Jonny played the Pachelbel canon and "Jesu Joy of Man's Desiring" on the guitar and you opened presents—a compass to guide you, a book—stories of spirit journeys, a fancy pocketknife, and a Native American medicine bag that held special charms. Dad put in his sweet bird of youth necklace; Jonny, a miniature dream catcher and a harmony ball; me, a tiny bag of beans—nourishment to grow and multiply or, in a pinch, keep you from starvation.

We shared stories and photographs of your birth and childhood. I made your favorite cake, a yeasty coffee cake topped with cherry and pineapple and squiggles of glazed frosting. The presents were wrapped in overlapping grape leaves, tied with long grasses, decorated with wild violets and a red rose. After you finished opening everything, you took the leaves and flowers, knelt by the side of the creek and set them floating downstream, watching until they were out of sight.

We all held hands and sat in silence for a time, then voiced our love, blessings, hopes and prayers for your path to come. It felt very satisfying, full of significance and symbol. But in retrospect, I see a huge missing piece. We inadvertently robbed you of something very important, Josh.

The passage from childhood to adult is more than privilege. It is something you earn from your elders as they lay the tribal mantle of history and responsibility upon your shoulders. And whether the mantle is adorned with temple bells, eagle feathers or tzitzit prayer knots, something is exacted; a test that makes sweat collect. Not the sweet damp of childhood, but a dank mushroomy odor sprung from a dark place of fear, unexplored appetites, from straining to meet the mark. In Hebrew schools, hogans, forests, churches, on walkabouts and mountaintops, young people are grilled on their scholarship of the law; their survival skills in the wilderness; their endurance of pain as they undergo circumcision or scarification. Where was the feeling that you had earned your manhood by the alchemy of your newly changed sweat? Was the pain you missed the reason you had an Essene Tree of Life burned into the muscling of your arm? And you, Jonny, the om mantra seared into each wrist? How could we have cheated you with the ease of privilege?

And which is more blinding? Flashed insight, or the fervor of every day?

Chapter 11

ZIMZUM

A STEADY STREAM OF FRIENDS and relatives file into the synagogue. The nervous, beaming mother and father of the bar mitzvah boy, Seymour-Uncle-Itzzy's, are already seated: Netchie in a navy satin dress with embroidered sleeves and a shoulder corsage of carnations, Itzzy in a dark suit, bow tie and boutonniere. Faye, their daughter, is in lavender chiffon. Aunts and uncles arrive all dressed in their Sabbath best, young girls in taffeta and satin sashes, small boys in belted sailor suits with short pants and white socks and shoes, and Anna in her new T-strap patent-leather shoes.

Wide-eyed, she walks down the wine-colored aisle carpet with her family. She is so enthralled by the muffled hush of the carpet beneath their feet, the high windows reflecting spates of sunlight onto walls and faces, the everlasting light glowing next to the Holy Ark on the pulpit, the soft organ music, she hardly notices all the people to whom her family smiles and

The whole mishpocheh, in its finery,

assembled around the bar mitzvah boy.

nods as they make their way to their seats. She is fascinated with the tall shadows they cast as they move through the bright patches of light. A shadow, she thinks, is a more believable image of a person than a body, for it grows and shrinks in response to time, place and light.

As Ben, Lisa and all their children settle into the aura of perfume, aftershave and corsages around them, Anna shifts her focus to the many faces. Here, with their families, sit the six sons of Shimin and Chana: her father Ben, Morris, Mike, Itzzy, Berney and Robert. A warm flush of realization seeps through Anna, a knowing that she belongs to all these people, and they to her. She remembers a similar feeling long ago when she was four—sleeping that day by the lake with Olga and Vasil after Grandmother Lochotsky died, when the earth took her safely into its bosom.

The congregation stills, intent on the black-robed rabbi and the thirteen-year-old boy who take their places on the pulpit.

"You studied well, Seymour," the rabbi says, patting him on the shoulder. "On your bar mitzvah you become a Son of the Commandments. In the community, you take your place as a man. Now go read your portion of the Torah with all your heart, with all your soul and with all your might."

"Yes, Rabbi," Seymour says. Together they walk to the ark and open the doors. The rabbi removes the Torah, the living, breathing body of Jewish law, caressed like a loved one, whirled as a partner in dance during shtetl weddings, buried and mourned if desecrated or burned. He hands the scrolls covered with gold-stitched silk to Seymour, who ceremoniously receives them, light as a child, heavy as history. The

Torah is undressed, unrolled and the silver pointer placed in Seymour's hand. Well schooled, he begins reading this day's portion, the Hebrew words from the thirty-third chapter of Exodus, long after the Jews have been delivered from oppression.

And Moses said, I beseech thee shew me thy glory. And the Lord said, I will make all my goodness pass before thee, and He said, Thou canst not see my face for there shall no man see me, and live.

Seymour looks up and sees the rapt expressions of his family—his luminous father and mother, hands tightly joined, who skidded to America over the frozen Dniester River; his beaming aunts and uncles and cousins.

Their faces are flames burning brighter and brighter, their lives ablaze with unbearable heat.

They are choking in the smoke-filled basement of Tetiev; suffocating with chaff under Yossip's barn floor; struggling for air through manure-plugged nostrils. A searing boil balloons on their ankles, bursts open and weeps; ice like fire cauterizes their blood. Their lungs are bursting.

Seymour cannot see faces anymore: all is consumed in one blinding light. And in that moment, in the midst of the conflagration, he sees the human face of God. Sees that it is love.

And he steps into the flames and breathes.

THE END AND THE

BEGINNING

Leaf shadows dance on the kitchen walls in the burnished afternoon light. The rich aroma of borscht, simmered since this morning in Grandpa Morris's pot, permeates the air.

This is your story, Josh and Jonny. Your people, your heritage, the soup of your blood. May it feed you and give you strength and joy on your own journey. And though I cannot protect you from the flames, I will always be here with the burn ointment. And with all my love.

Jonny and Josh

A c k n o w l e d g m e n t s

The joke goes, "So what is the speed of dark?"

The speed of light, on the other hand, is discernible. You can see how far-reaching, powerful and illuminating it is when you try to convey thanks for a story like this.

Unfathomable gratitude to Jack Axelrood. Without *The Brothers Axelrood: Their Story,* written in 1969 by Jack (Jackie, in this story), *The Soup Has Many Eyes* would be an empty soup pot. His history of the Axelrood family is the foundation for this book. Like Jack, I called on members of the family for their recollections. His is a true story and can be found at the Library of Congress. This, too, is a true story, however transformed by imagined encounters, words and chronological uncertainties.

To Seymour, who urged Jack to write about the Axelrood family.

To my son, Joshua, who after reading Elie Wiesel's *Night* wanted to know about our family and ravenously devoured this story page by page, as fast as I could write it.

To my son, Jonny, my wellspring, who runs quiet and deep, for his clarity of insight and his abiding support.

To my husband, Bob, for all things, in all ways.

To Simmy Makhijani, Josh's friend, who read this and followed her own story to India. She, like Josh, encouraged bringing these words to the wider world and showed me how hungry our young people are to hear of those who came before them, and how much story there is to be shared between generations.

To Sylvia Rose, my mother, who continues to give me recipes for soup, courage, serenity and persistence.

To Frances Goldin, my agent and my cousin (this is her story too), for her expertise and wisdom, and for a life lived in extraordinary and compassionate action in the cause of justice.

To Richard Axelrood, Cynthia Glickman, Bruce Gordon, Amy Jannelli, Ann Marks and Rachel Povereny for sharing memories and photographs.

To my foremothers and forefathers who came in a heartbeat and patiently endured countless interruptions to guide this story.

To Trudy Lipowsky (the second generation of survivors of the Holocaust) for vetting the Yiddish, Mary Rohrer-Dann for treasured friendship and support as well as her keenly tuned writer's ear, and Dan Walden for his scholarship and guidance.

To Blossom Aberg, Dan Carter, Helen and Lowell Manfull, Rickie Moore, Shar Marbury and Gigi Marino for reading and improving these pages.

To Jack McManis, John Haag and Paul West, my magnificent teachers along the way.

And most especially, to Ann Harris, my incredible editor/collaborator at Bantam, who has been a loving, guiding and exquisitely perceptive mother to this story. Like a mother, she helped raise these words from infancy, nudged them into lucidity and opened the door of opportunity for their journey.